T0366854

Preventing Crises at Your University

Preventing Crises at Your University

The Playbook for Protecting Your Institution's Reputation

Simon R. Barker

Johns Hopkins University Press · *Baltimore*

Johns Hopkins University Press
2715 North Charles Street
Baltimore, Maryland 21218-4363
www.press.jhu.edu

Library of Congress Cataloging-in-Publication Data

Names: Barker, Simon R., 1969- author.
Title: Preventing crises at your university : the playbook for protecting
    your institution's reputation / Simon R. Barker.
Description: Baltimore : Johns Hopkins University Press, 2021. | Includes
    bibliographical references and index.
Identifiers: LCCN 2021017888 | ISBN 9781421442679 (paperback ; acid-free
    paper) | ISBN 9781421442686 (ebook)
Subjects: LCSH: Universities and colleges—Ratings and rankings—United States. |
    Educational indicators—United States. | Educational leadership—United States. |
    Schools—Risk management—United States. | Reputation.
Classification: LB2331.63 .B37 2021
LC record available at https://lccn.loc.gov/2021017888

A catalog record for this book is available from the British Library.

Illustrations are by Mircea Sinpetru.

*Special discounts are available for bulk purchases of this book. For more information,
please contact Special Sales at specialsales@jh.edu.*

Contents

Preface

"There cannot be a crisis next week. My schedule is already full" is one of many famous quotes attributed to Henry Kissinger. For most leaders in higher education, this sentiment no doubt rings true, and particularly during this last year: the pandemic, budget and financial woes, contentious politics and social issues spilling over into campuses. For me, this quote also explains the incredibly long gestation period of this book, which began approximately ten years ago, with intermittent progress constantly interrupted by crises at higher education institutions large and small.

That's my excuse for why this book wasn't written earlier. Those intervening years, however, have contributed significantly to the content, substance, and insight I hope readers will glean from it. This book is truly a product of collaboration, constant learning, and taking on board the wise words of those with whom I have had the honor and joy of working over these years. Among the many I could mention, I would like first to acknowledge the influence of Bob Wilkerson, whom I first met at Marsh and McLennan in 2008. Bob, a pioneer in the field of crisis management in the 1980s, brought a rigor, discipline, and methodology to the entire field. Today, I remain constantly thankful for his insight, amazed by his encyclopedic knowledge on almost every conceivable topic, and appreciative of his gentle wisdom and guidance.

Second, I would like to posthumously thank Michael Deaver, whom I worked with at Edelman in Washington, DC, for four years in the late 1990s. He had an uncanny ability to get to the heart of any strategic issue within a matter of minutes, and instilled a confidence in clients that, whatever was going on, there was a route through. Without him taking me under his wing, I doubt highly I would ever have had the confidence to support and guide organizations in the middle of significant crises. I continue to aspire to have something approximating his insight, influence, and presence.

Finally, and most importantly, I want to thank my wife and partner in life, love, adventure, and business—Jen Rettig. Jen has truly been my inspiration and the impetus throughout my life and my career—from moving us from Hawaii to Washington, DC, so that I could get "real" crisis experience, to getting an MBA at Cornell. She gave me the courage and confidence for us to start Blue Moon Consulting Group together—even with no clients, no savings, and our two children, Aidan and Alex, only a few years from going to university themselves.

Throughout our life together, Jen has always challenged my assumptions and pushed me to strengthen and crystalize nascent ideas into robust concepts. I know she truly has my back and is always interested in making me a better person, and, as she knows better than anyone, there is lots of room for improvement there. No doubt this book would have been quite different—and certainly not as strong and clear—without her encouragement, ideas, and critical thinking. In fact, without her, it likely would not have been written at all.

So, please take a few hours out of your hectic schedules to read this book. I hope it is informative, mildly entertaining, and most importantly, useful to you as you navigate the inevitable issues and crises that may lie ahead.

Thank you.

Preventing Crises at Your University

Introduction

Mind the Gap: Why Reputational Risk Matters

"Mind the Gap" is a well-known warning for anyone who has traveled on the London Underground; it cautions any unsuspecting riders that there might be a gap between the platform and the doors of the carriage they are about to board or to leave. The gap, however, can be terrifying, particularly for an uninitiated traveler—easily able to swallow a small stroller—and is a typical British understatement of risk.

This book is about the need to "mind the gap" between the generally positive association leaders of higher education have with the importance of reputation and the generally negative and ill-informed perception they may have about ways to protect against reputational damage or reputational risk. This disconnect can be alarmingly wide and needs to be narrowed considerably if universities and colleges want to maintain their right to operate and protect their institution's most valuable, intangible asset: its reputation; or, to continue the analogy, both board the train and make it to their destination safely.

The long-lasting nature of the stakeholder relationships in higher education should create a shared understanding that building and protecting an institution's reputation is core to the strategy of the institution. Many leaders in higher education, however, have a complex relationship with the entire concept of "reputation."

On one hand, reputation is a convenient shorthand for all that is positive about their institution—the quality of the academic instruction and research led by faculty; the achievements of its students; the success of its athletic programs, the engagement and support from its alumni, its "town and gown" relationships, and so on. Leaders also recognize that the reputation of their institution can be significantly damaged by a poorly managed issue or crisis on their campus.

On the other hand, discussing the concept of how to build and protect reputation is viewed as a little tawdry. "Managing" reputation seems dishonest, essentially counterproductive, undermining the concept of reputation in the first place—shouldn't reputation just be an organic outcome of reality? The oft-used phrase "perception is reality," which often seems to get bandied around at times when discussing reputation, also only undermines the strategic value of proactively considering reputation, reducing it to "smoke and mirrors." Many university presidents have said—in the middle of a crisis—that they aren't going to make a specific decision because of "concerns about reputation." *Reputation* in this context is used as a pejorative; a dirty word that is viewed as undermining leadership credibility and the values of the institution.

How is it possible that reputation can be almost uniformly agreed to be critical to ongoing success for any institution and yet, at the same time, protecting reputation is typically viewed as inherently distasteful and counterproductive? At its heart, this book is about closing the gap between the generally recognized importance and value of reputation and the generally discounted or maligned approaches to "managing" reputational risk. Typically, it is only at the time of a crisis that "reputational risk" suddenly becomes a very real issue for administrative leaders, as they struggle to maintain their authority to lead and their right to operate. That is too late.

The need to close the gap between these contrary impulses has also accelerated because of the complexities inherent in higher education today, because of societal factors as well as institutional complexity and fragmentation. When we think about a college or university, we tend to think primarily about the classroom experience. While clearly foundational, the classroom is where only a sliver of the activity at many universities today occurs, under the umbrella of which can be included:

- Academic medical centers, as well as related multi-billion-dollar hospitals and health care systems, which can frequently be larger than the host institution with which they share a name and often governance
- Research enterprises that attract hundreds of millions of dollars of federal, philanthropic, and corporate investment
- International campuses and a plethora of cobranded and affiliated programs
- Athletic programs and, specifically, football programs, which are almost autonomous from campus operations, generating millions of dollars in revenue or, more typically, losses

The size and scope of the institution is a challenge compounded by a risk that applies to both large universities and small colleges: institutional fragmentation. Fragmentation takes many forms, including:

- The leading business school that does not view itself as part of the main campus
- The tenured academic who has little to no "loyalty" to the institution and stoutly stands behind academic freedom as sufficient rationale for anything

- The researcher who believes herself to be so brilliant that constraints on inappropriate research do not apply
- The football team that decides to form a separate legal entity to reduce future legal liability, yet remains deeply enmeshed in the culture of the institution
- The summer program for high schoolers that uses the facilities and brand of the institution but otherwise has little affiliation

While authority and responsibility may be fragmented, accountability remains centralized, as does reputational risk. When something goes wrong, wherever and whatever the cause, the reputation of the entire institution can be damaged.

Higher education as a sector is in a unique place: a complex set of competitive, political, financial, and social challenges; a sometimes distended and fragmented management structure; uniquely personal and lasting relationship with stakeholders; and a reputation that is at a crossroads. As at any junction, there are a number of options. Keep heading in the same direction in the same way is certainly an option, albeit unlikely to end in a different place.

Typically, no one is responsible for managing reputational risk. At most institutions, there is no defined program or budget or staff to further the goals of protecting an institution's reputation. There are rarely defined objectives or performance criteria against which to understand whether an institution's reputation is more at risk than it was the year before. When reputational risk is nebulous and is everyone's responsibility, it essentially becomes no one's responsibility.

If it is no one's responsibility—or perhaps added nonchalantly to the president's list of things to worry about—is it any surprise that it is not proactively managed? It should also not be a surprise that most institutions view reputational risk as essentially unmanageable—some type of accidental by-product, akin to an uncontrolled tailpipe emission. To some degree, this is the central problem that needs to be tackled. When there are insufficient management tools, methodology, or even language to describe what needs to be in place in order to manage and mitigate reputational risk, is it a surprise that it is not being managed at all?

The one exception is when reputational risk is delegated to the public relations or media relations team in a school's marketing and communications function. Although communications specialists have some important parts of the skill set required to effectively manage reputational risk, theirs is a very limited view as to what is required. Reputational risk—while certainly about the way an institution is perceived, and thus communications is a critical component—is not fundamentally a communications challenge. Reputational risk is a strategic risk that can only be mitigated when managed strategically: integrated with the broader strategy of the institution, reflective of institutional values, and driving a culture in which reputational risk is proactively identified, mitigated, and managed.

The goal of this book, therefore, is to suggest that a renewed focus and rigorous approach to managing reputational risk is vital not only for individual institutions but also for higher education as a whole. It requires five distinct steps:

1. Develop a clearer understanding of what reputation is and how to protect it in an increasingly complex, connected, and challenging environment.
2. Define the capabilities needed to protect institutional reputation, including a mindset and series of management processes that are sufficiently robust to proactively identify and mitigate reputational risk.
3. Align institutional values with decision-making when facing significant issues or crises.
4. Establish a new crisis leadership model appropriate for self-inflicted and reputational crises, as opposed to the typical over-focus on physical emergencies.
5. Incorporate new management frameworks that can be applied to a school of any size to ensure a more concerted,

progressively mature, and capable approach to managing reputational risk.

It is only once these steps have been taken that an institution's reputation, and the credibility of its leadership team, will be protected—by having the capability to identify and mitigate issues before they become a crisis, respond effectively during a crisis, and meet the evolving expectations of the variety of stakeholders on which the institution relies upon for its ongoing success.

Chapter 1

A Reputational Risk Framework

The way to gain a good reputation is to endeavor to be what you desire to appear.

—Socrates

Defining Reputation and Why It Is at Risk

Before we can go much further to understand what "reputational risk" means and what an institution can do to proactively manage it, we first need to have a better understanding of what we mean by reputation. Twenty-five hundred years ago, Socrates stated that the way to gain a good reputation is to endeavor to be what you desire to appear to be. The reputation of an individual seller in a marketplace could rise and fall with the quality and price of the products and services offered, his willingness to work with his customers when things go wrong, and more generally, the value of those products and services to the broader community. The close relationship between buyer and seller, between the individual and the community in the marketplace of Socrates' time, had the potential to create a virtuous circle, in which a good reputation would lead to increased business and reward, and conversely, a bad reputation would result in lost business or status in society. The simplicity of the feedback loop created a belief that responsible citizenship was possible and that reputation was fundamental.

Ever since modern corporations took shape in the seventeenth century and were vested with similar rights and obligations as individuals, Socrates' definition of reputation has been applied to organizations as well. But is it relevant? On face value, it appears that the feedback loop and the proximity between buyers and sellers in the Athenian marketplace has been transformed into a global marketplace with only loose, transactional relationships, and unpredictably applied punishment for those organizations that do not "endeavor to be what they desire to appear" or reward for those that do.

For higher education, however, the strong ties between institution and stakeholders have made this concept of reputation more salient and relevant than it is, in general, in the corporate world.

- The bonds between students and their school can be profound, defining, in part, who students are as individuals, the friends they have, the careers they follow, and the long-term relationship with their alma mater through homecomings and class reunions.
- The ties between a community and its university are also typically deep and long-lasting—entire communities either built around an institution or contributing significantly to the cultural and economic life and opportunities of the location—and typically share a common name.
- The tradition of tenured faculty means a lasting commitment to the institution, the students, and their colleagues beyond any typical employer-employee model in a business environment.

As strong as the enduring ties between a university or college and its key stakeholders are, living up to that bond is becoming increasingly difficult due to new technologies and changing societal dynamics.

Social Media

For the first time, technology has created a set of powerful tools that can recreate the sense of the old marketplace in today's global economy, with social media networks bringing it all together. Those with shared interests are connected in a way that means the whole is greater than the sum of its parts.

Nothing goes without notice or comment. TikTok, Twitter, and YouTube drive revolutions. Experiences, good and bad, are telegraphed via Yelp, Tripadvisor, Glassdoor, and—especially pertinent to higher ed—Rate My Professors. As demonstrated by Wikileaks, any confidential internal document can be leaked and made available to anyone who cares enough about your institution to investigate. Powerful search engines like Google mean that despite the vast amount of information, both useful and just noise, anyone can find all the information—or misinformation—they want about anything. Social media, discussed in chapter 7, has fundamentally changed both the challenges of protecting an institution's reputation and the importance of doing so.

A Trust Deficit

As catalogued over the years by the Edelman Trust Barometer and other research, trust among almost all the formal institutions of power—government, business, religion, and the media—is at low levels. Whether a cause or effect of social media can be debated but is less important than the fact that people are highly skeptical of all official information sources, which continues to give outsized credibility and credence to the "unfiltered" and "genuine" information one gets from social media. While this dynamic has shifted considerably in the last few years, with trust in social media companies (particularly Facebook) falling dramatically, owing to its inability or unwillingness to prevent or flag "fake news," its cumulative effect is a decline in trust of information that does not match preexisting attitudes or, as is discussed in chapter 7, align with "the prevailing narrative."

Academia is a relative bright spot and is typically viewed more highly than the other formal institutions of power. However, that trust normally applies to individual professors, not "the administration" of the same institution. The ivory tower simply isn't what it used to be.

This "trust deficit" in society at large is particularly challenging for any organization's attempt to mitigate reputational risk. Frequently, social media, rumor, and innuendo are given far more credibility and weight than official pronouncements. The typically asymmetric nature of the level of detail an institution can provide (whether due to legal concerns, on-going investigations, or simply fealty to provable facts) seems scarce and unpersuasive compared to the information and detail shared by critics. Conspiracy theories abound. The polarized media environment reduces everything to polemic, and the news is more about finding facts that support existing values or positions than challenging them or seeking the truth. An environment in which the distinction between fact-based news and opinion is increasingly blurred further makes for an uphill battle for any school that needs to explain itself.

An Industry under Fire

This trust deficit in higher education is caused by broad questions about affordability, accessibility, equity, and impact in ways that higher education hasn't faced before. These broad "industry" challenges are exacerbated by poorly managed crises—whether systemic challenges concerning sexual assault (particularly when overlooked by academic and athletic leaders); protests and sit-ins on topics from freedom of speech, racism, animal rights, to tuition and divestment; the role of "legacy" candidates and, more broadly, privilege and bribery in admission decisions; or more prosaically, broader societal issues from which higher education is not immune, such as increasing disparity of pay between administration leaders and athletic coaches and the frontline staff who deliver the educational "product"— teaching assistants and adjunct faculty. The idea of and support for education as "a public good" is declining.*

Given the importance of reputation to higher education, the array of risks unique to higher education and the broader array of societal issues for which higher education is often the crucible (environmental issues, racial and gender issues, economic equity, etc.), the lack of focus on reputational risk is both cause and effect for the self-inflicted damage institutions cause to their reputations.

Reputation needs to be regarded less as a nebulous concept or omnipresent force, which as a result is completely unmanageable, to being viewed as a critical intangible asset, valued and protected in the same way as is intellectual property. Given the profound risks institutions of higher education face in today's environment, it is virtually a dereliction of a board's fiduciary duty or the administration's leadership team to believe that reputational risk is either something that just happens and is impossible to manage or, equally problematically, is a problem that "communications" can fix. Understanding what places an institution's reputation at risk is significantly more complicated than understanding an individual's reputation. It is also significantly more important to do so.

Understanding Reputational Risk

While Socrates' definition of reputation is both prosaic and aspirational, more recent frequently used quotes about reputation have focused on the risk of damaging reputation: Benjamin Franklin stating, "It takes many good deeds to build a good reputation, and only one bad one to lose it;" Warren Buffet, the business "Sage of Omaha," claiming, "It takes twenty years to

*The Association of Public & Land-Grant Universities Survey: "How Covid Changed Everything and Nothing," June 2020.

build a reputation and five minutes to ruin it. If you think about that, you'll do things differently." These famous quotes focus on the fragility of an organization's reputation.

So, what is an appropriate way to define reputational risk? I define it as follows:

> Reputational Risk occurs when there is a significant disconnect between an organization's decisions and the expectations of its stakeholders.

Or, in Socrates' parlance, you "fail to be what you desire to appear." Reputational risk is highest during a crisis, but slow-evolving, unaddressed issues can be as corrosive over time as any crisis and result in potential long-term and sometimes unrecoverable damage.

It is because of the nebulous quality of reputational risk that little attention beyond lip-service is paid by institutions of higher education, in general, to understanding their reputation, what drives it, and what contribution it makes to the institution's success and long-term viability, with two exceptions: rankings and brand.

Rankings, without getting into the details of multiple concerns regarding changes in methodology or the self-fulfilling nature of some of the criteria (such as selectivity), it could be argued, is the closest proxy for reputation. Rankings criteria are broad and encompass multiple components of the university experience and success, from citations as a proxy for academic excellence, retention rates for the student experience, job placement and earnings for overall quality of education, strength of alumni networks, and so on. Due to their increasing prominence in enrollment campaigns, most institutions carefully manage the submittal process to rankings organizations, or some may even change their underlying institutional strategy to gain some marginal gain in rankings criteria.

Brand management, pioneered in the corporate environment in the mid-1960s and now commonplace, is a relatively new concept in higher education, a trend that has accelerated over the last fifteen to twenty years. Schools across the country are supporting increasingly sophisticated and expensive branding campaigns in order to help differentiate their institutions in a crowded and competitive marketplace. Brand is frequently used as a substitute for reputation or conflated with reputation in a way to suggest that there is no meaningful difference. And while brand can support and strengthen institutional reputation, the two are not the same.

While at an aggregated level, most schools have strong brands and arguably vulnerable reputations, this is not inevitable. Protecting a reputation requires two things: (1) a more rigorous and

Understanding the Distinction: Brand versus Reputation

Brand is stated. Brand is the story you tell about yourself. It may draw from your history or it may be more aspirational, signaling to your community a strategic direction. Traditionally, in higher education, brand and marketing efforts are oriented toward a limited number of stakeholders, principally prospective students and parents for enrollment campaigns and alumni and donors as part of fundraising and capital campaigns. Brand, in general, is well funded and well managed by your marketing and communications teams. Brand should also be considered a leading indicator of where the institution aspires to be and is heading.

Reputation is earned. In contrast, reputation is the complete picture of your institution built up over decades, if not centuries. It is based on the actions and behaviors of every person associated with your school: your researchers, your student-athletes, your alumni, and even your founders. Reputation encompasses the perspective of all stakeholders—alumni, current students and faculty, vendors, regulators, and even local communities. In this regard, reputation is typically a slow-moving and lagging indicator—who the institution has been—and so sometimes institutional reputation is undeserved.

thoughtful approach regarding the capabilities and processes necessary to manage reputational risk; and (2) a rebalancing of the institutional focus and time spent on building versus protecting institutional reputation.

If universities and colleges paid the same careful attention to understanding and protecting their institutional reputation as they do to building their brand, then schools would be in a better position to mitigate reputational risk. This is not to suggest this is a zero-sum game. Rather, building a capability and approach to manage reputational risk is an investment in the same way a hedge or derivative is used to protect the value of the underlying asset. All of the work, time, and money spent on building brand equity can potentially be undone by one major issue or crisis, which can have dramatic and sudden impacts on an institution's reputation and its relationship with key stakeholders.

Risk Management

In today's environment, leaders need to change their perspective on reputational risk—from it being nebulous and essentially unmanageable to treating it as an organization's most valuable, and fragile, intangible asset. The challenge, however, is that approaches to managing reputational risk are either insufficient, piecemeal, or poorly defined and understood within the organization.

The good news is that components of a proactive reputational risk framework do exist—at some level—in most institutions of higher education, but they need to be properly defined and understood, built together and aligned, and importantly, support the overarching strategy and competitive advantages of the institution. The promise of a proactive reputational risk management framework is that the institution will be in a position to:

- identify the risks and issues that threaten its viability;
- manage crises when they do occur;

- create the reservoir of goodwill among multiple stakeholders it requires to have the time necessary to adapt and continue to thrive; and
- provide a fundamental strategic advantage to the institution in today's highly critical, social media driven, skeptical environment.

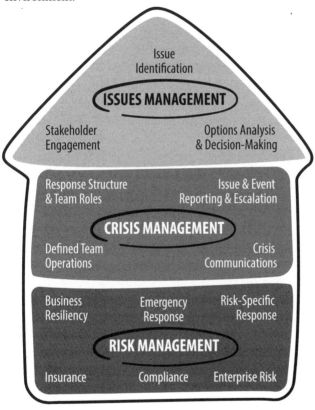

Reputational Risk Management Framework. The reputational risk management framework comprises three fundamental capabilities, which together provide the ability to manage reputational risk. These components not only build on each other but also reflect an increasing level of sophistication, maturity, and capability in an organization's approach. Chapters 4-7 and 9 discuss in detail the requirements needed to develop the component capabilities described here.

Unfortunately, in most schools, very little is in place outside of the basic risk management functions—those at the base of the framework in the illustration. The most common are compliance programs to assess adherence to policies designed to limit and manage operational risk; insurance policies to offset the financial costs should something go wrong; and then emergency response—typically managed by public safety or police departments—to respond when it does. However, typically focused on active shooter risk and natural or manmade disruptions and disasters (earthquake, tornado, hurricane or utility failure, chemical release, etc.), emergency response is not the same as crisis response. This important distinction—which is often an area for confusion and misunderstanding at universities and colleges—is discussed in detail in chapter 5.

Other components of the risk management level tend to be less robust.

Enterprise risk management (a systemic way to identify, prioritize, and manage risk) is relatively unknown in most academic institutions, although that situation is improving.

Business resiliency, or "mission continuity," as it is sometimes referred to, is typically limited to disaster recovery of IT functions and sometimes to relocation of classes and students in the case of a building becoming unavailable. Most schools at the height of their COVID-19 pandemic planning quickly recognized that whatever they did have in place to enable both effective work-from-home strategies for staff or remote learning options were woefully inadequate, and a great deal had to be built on the fly.

Risk-specific response refers to a plethora of potential plans that an institution may have developed over time to address unique risk areas, most typically cyber risk or data breach plans and behavioral threat assessment.

While the components in a comprehensive risk management approach should certainly merit some focus, the highest priority, particularly in the context of managing reputational risk, is the absence of a properly defined and understood approach to crisis management or any kind of proactive, strategic issues management program at most institutions. Before providing an overview of a crisis management capability or an issues management capability, it is first vital to define terms that are often confused and poorly defined.

The Difference between an Issue and a Crisis

One of the earliest books on crisis management defines a crisis as "a serious threat to the basic structures or the fundamental values and norms of a system, which under time pressure and highly uncertain circumstances necessitates making vital decisions."* Another way to think about a crisis is as a threat to your organization in which events are unfolding rapidly, accurate information is scarce, and the pressure to respond is high.

Three qualities need to be present for a situation to be viewed as a crisis:

1. *Threat.* The issue or event has to pose a significant threat to the institution and risk damaging its people, facilities, service, or reputation. A threat can be physical—such as an active shooter or a tornado—or it can be reputational—such as allegations of financial fraud, abuse or misuse of power, sexual assault, racism, etc.
2. *Uncertainty.* A threat itself is not sufficient to become a crisis. There has to be uncertainty caused by lack of information

*Argen Boin, Paul 't Hart, Eric Stern, and Bengt Sundelius, *The Politics of Crisis Management: Public Leadership under Pressure* (Cambridge: Cambridge University Press, 2005).

Defining a Crisis

about what is actually going on (as is often the case in fast-moving situations) or lack of clarity about what the right decision needs to be (sometimes related to the first); but a "right" answer is not always apparent. A crisis often presents leadership with two bad options, each with risks and benefits that need to be quickly identified and compared. If there is a threat but no uncertainty regarding strategic decision-making (that is, it is clear what needs to be done), the situation is not a crisis.

3. *Urgency.* The final quality that needs to be present for a situation to be a crisis is the lack of time or the need for urgent response, decision-making, and communication. This is the hardest part of effective crisis management, particularly for leaders in higher education who cherish dialog and debate and value calm deliberation and assessment of data before making a decision—luxuries that are never present in a crisis.

If the combination of threat, uncertainty, and urgency constitutes a crisis, what is an issue? The main difference between an issue and a crisis is this absence of urgency, which can be both a blessing and a curse. It can be a blessing as it allows the institution time to make more measured decisions—to evaluate the risks and uncertainties in a more deliberate and analytical way. You have time to develop a more coherent and consistent communications strategy and to explain to stakeholders the steps your institution is taking and why.

While it depends on the severity of the issue, all too frequently, because of the lack of urgency, an issue gets put on the back burner. Unlike a crisis, there is frequently no defined, cross-functional team assigned to mitigate the risk, and there are no goals or milestones to meet. Ultimately, nothing gets done. That does not mean the issue has been resolved; rather, it has been deprioritized and will frequently fester until it has metastasized, and it is too late. A related event or incident occurs, and stakeholders—and eventually the media—begin to demand concrete action and clear information. Now a crisis, the previously manageable issue leaves the administration looking reactive and lacking sufficient control. Leadership credibility is compromised, and the issue is compounded. Like a crisis, the perceived (in)effectiveness of the response can have more influence on reputation than the issue itself.

Defining Crisis Management

Crisis management would on the face of it seem a fairly clear term. However, it often gets confused and co-opted. Similar terms *disaster, emergency, incident* should and actually do mean different things but are often jumbled up, either on purpose or out of laziness.

One of the most common mistakes in higher education is to equate emergency management with crisis management. Emergency management defines the process to manage specific physical *events*, such as an active shooter or a natural disaster. Crisis management defines the process to manage the broader *impacts* and *consequences* of a full range of events and issues, not just physical ones. Emergency management is important. However, on its own it is insufficient. Based on a typical university's risk profile and the fact that 90 percent of crises are driven by reputational risk, emergency response is typically overemphasized. This is discussed further in chapter 4.

A second mistake is to equate crisis communication with crisis management—how the institution communicates to its stakeholders, typically with a specific focus on media, at a time of significant external negative scrutiny. Certainly, poor crisis management is almost guaranteed when Communications is not at the table when decisions are being made, leaving Communications with the job of "explaining" potentially poor decisions that will not withstand stakeholder scrutiny. On the other hand, ineffective, inaccurate, or incomplete communications can undermine an institution's credibility, even if the basic response and strategy are appropriate.

While communications certainly is a critical, visible, and impactful part of crisis management, it should not be mistaken for the whole. This limited understanding of crisis management assumes that (1) nothing much was or could have been done to prevent the situation from escalating into a crisis situation in the first place; or that (2) effective communication is going to solve the problem. A press release isn't going to solve this, only action can.

Higher education is not alone in poorly defining crisis management. In the corporate sector, crisis management is often limited to the process necessary to coordinate response to a disaster or business continuity event or, more recently, is used interchangeably with cyber-incident response. In health care, crisis response plans often refer to providing immediate psychological counseling to victims of traumatic events. Other organizations take a page out of the military playbook and have crisis "black-ops" teams, even if what they are actually dealing with is logistics for a large conference. As a core component of effective reputational risk management, crisis management must be properly understood and defined.

What, then, is an appropriate definition of crisis management, as distinct from emergency management?

> Crisis management is a senior-level management process that allows on organization to make fast, coordinated, and proactive decisions regarding a comprehensive set of risks that can withstand the credibility test of intense stakeholder scrutiny. It provides a defined process that—through its prompt and tangible incorporation of stakeholder concerns into decision-making— has the potential to prevent an incident from becoming a crisis in the first place and protects the credibility of the management team and the overall reputation of the organization.

Defining Issues Management

If crisis management is frequently poorly defined, issues management is even more fundamentally misunderstood. Instead of being viewed as a strategic tool, the term itself conveys a deviousness or sleight of hand, "spin" used to confuse rather than to educate, a reactive process to put the best face on the issue of the day. In many cases, that is all it is. It ends up being about trying to construct a credible explanation to minimize criticism and increase support for an institution's position, policy, or course of action—however poorly considered. This is part of the explanation for many leader's skepticism about the value or ethics of "protecting reputation."

If issues management is to provide valuable strategic insight to your leadership team, however, it cannot simply be about rationalizing preordained positions. To be effective, the approach must be aligned with institutional values, address the expectations of key stakeholders, and by so doing, explicitly incorporate reputational criteria as a key variable in decision-making. Operating at the intersection of an institution and its stakeholders, a disciplined and rigorous approach to issues management should be at the heart of any program designed to understand, build, and protect an institution's reputation. It has two distinct roles: (1) to incorporate stakeholder expectations into decision-making; and (2) to increase understanding of the organization's goals and values among those stakeholders who are important to its long-term success.

So what is an appropriate definition of issues management?

Issues management is the process to identify, prioritize and systematically address issues that can have a significant but slowly-evolving or corrosive impact on the reputation and viability of the institution over time. It serves as an early-warning indicator and, through strategic changes or more effective communications, can prevent an issue from becoming a crisis.

Creating Options: The Issues-to-Crisis Continuum

Urgency, or perceived lack of it, is one way to distinguish between a crisis and an issue. Another way is to look at the decreasing range of options available to mitigate the risk.

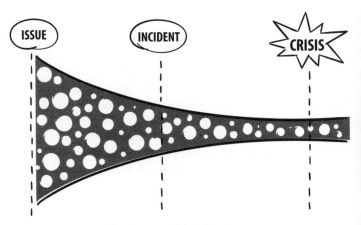

The Issues-to-Crisis Continuum

Issue. When an issue is identified, there is sufficient time and typically plenty of options on how to manage it. Programs can be advanced to reduce the saliency of the issue, policies can be changed or strengthened, and communications developed. With sufficient time, effort, and focus, effective issues management should prevent an issue from degenerating into a crisis.

Incident. An incident is a specific event or development that brings an issue to the foreground. While the range of options is more limited, early identification provides the administration a number of options to effectively manage it and, again, prevent the incident from degenerating into a crisis. If the incident relates to an already identified issue, most of the response required should already be in place.

Crisis. By the time we reach a crisis, the range of options is highly limited, typically to just two options, each often a bad choice, having significant negative impacts and consequences. Institutions typically reach the crisis point by failing to address an incident earlier enough (through appropriate reporting and escalation) or by having allowed an identified issue to remain unaddressed and fester.

The goal in developing a robust reputational risk management program is to create options, to buy time, and to prevent avoidable, self-inflicted crises from occurring. The administration should be pushed to intervene in a meaningful way both sooner and farther to the left along the issues-to-crisis continuum.

In summary, the reputational risk management framework defines the various constituent parts that every institution should have in place to increase its capability to manage reputational risk. Like every management process, this capability must build and mature over time, and it needs to be transformed from being an "initiative" or a "paper plan" to becoming embedded in the culture of the institution. As important, these distinct capabilities need to work together and align, something that is often difficult to achieve when they are "owned" by different parts of the institution—in those rare situations in which the components actually are in place.

For most universities and colleges, however, these capabilities are not in place. Many institutions are under the mistaken impression that mandated federal requirements for emergency response and some good communications skills are going to prove sufficient to manage reputational risk. They will not.

More than Values

Earlier we defined reputational risk as occurring "when there is a significant disconnect between an organization's decisions and the expectations of its stakeholders." What this boils down to is, essentially, a question of values—Has the institution acted in a way that is consistent with a general understanding of the values of the institution? These values may be explicit or inferred over time, based on responses to other issues or crises. In every instance, it is the seeming abandonment of values at a time of crisis that causes reputational damage.

At its heart, does the institution's leadership have a mindset that actively incorporates reputational risk into the decision-making process? This explains in part why many books on crisis tend to distill complex problems down to simplistic concepts such as "tell the truth" or "be transparent" or "apologize and demonstrate empathy" or "get ahead of the issue" or just "live your values"—as if that were as easily done as said.

While there is nothing inherently wrong with any of the above advice, establishing a process and a culture in an organization to enable an effective decision-making process to be achieved in the middle of a significant issue or crisis is challenging, and it requires a concerted organizational effort, as this book will address. The next chapter discusses what frequently goes wrong in a crisis—when reputational risk is at its most acute—before moving on to discuss tangible solutions to those challenges.

Chapter 2

Nine Things That Go Wrong in Crises

It takes twenty years to build a reputation and five minutes to ruin it. If you think about that, you'll do things differently.

—Warren Buffett

The single most important thing to understand about reputational risk is that the cause of a crisis is almost immaterial. Rather, the perception of the effectiveness of the response to the crisis is the largest determining factor of the impact on the reputation of an institution and how quickly, if ever, it recovers. This bears repeating—the perception of the effectiveness of the response to the crisis is more important to the reputation of an institution than the crisis itself.

This is good news. It means that through effective response to a crisis, it is possible to significantly limit its impact, and in fact in some instances, the institution can emerge stronger because of the way the crisis was handled; leadership credibility can be strengthened, and the reputation of the institution can be burnished. Crisis management is not a zero-sum game—it is possible to achieve more than just survival.

That said, before going further into the key components of effective crisis management—the ones that need to be in place to give the institution a chance to manage the crisis—it is important to discuss the things that most often go wrong. None of the components of effective crisis management—issues identification, response structure, team operations, and crisis communications, which will be detailed in the following chapters—are developed for their own sake but rather because they can help prevent "unforced errors" at the time of a crisis.

It is important always to remember that crisis management needs to be designed to solve the actual challenges and issues that organizations face when in the middle of a crisis. Fundamentally, crisis management is not an oxymoron but is actually achievable, if we recognize the challenges and build an aligned capability to manage reputational risk.

Challenge 1: Finding Out about the Problem Too Late

It is human nature to either deny that something has gone wrong or believe it can easily be resolved. It is also human nature, when the risk is unavoidable, to either transfer blame or to attempt to solve the problem in advance of reporting it; it is generally much more palatable to disclose, "We had a problem, but now it's fixed" than "We have a problem and we don't have an answer right now."

This natural human response to bad news typically means that the issues or incidents are not shared early enough, appropriate resources are not allocated quickly enough, and what could have been a manageable issue degenerates into a crisis for an institution, with reputational damage exacerbated by the perceived slowness to respond in the first place.

It is impossible to be proactive if you find out about a situation too late. "Why didn't we learn about this earlier?" is the typical question asked. The risk of potentially important information not being shared or escalated is compounded if someone believes that reporting bad news will result in a "shoot the messenger" response.

Challenge 2: Over-Optimism

Over-optimism manifests itself in three different ways:

1. As a failure to recognize that the institution is not uniquely positioned to withstand sector-wide issues
2. Once in a crisis, as a misplaced belief that things aren't as bad as they seem
3. An overconfidence in the ability of the team to get out of the crisis

Overly Optimistic Assessment of Risk. Despite the daily email reports from the *Chronicle of Higher Education* or *Inside Higher Ed* describing the half dozen or so institutions that are caught in the headlines for some type of institutional failure or another, it is still remarkable to hear, "Oh, that would never happen to us." The number of institutions, particularly in the Northeast, that are facing the so-called demographic cliff and yet believe that they have a unique value proposition and will be able to grow their enrollment as a way to solve systemic financial problems is astonishing.* There is, unfortunately, a Lake Woebegone, rose-tinted-spectacled view of risk at many institutions. We all want to believe the best about the institutions at which we work and the people with or for whom we work, but it is critical for institutions to have a shared and realistic view of the risks a crisis generates.

Even once the "it would never happen to us" is demonstrably no longer a viable response, there remains the tendency to want to believe that it is "not as bad as it seems" or "if we ignore

*Nathan D. Grawe, *Demographics and the Demand for Higher Education* (Baltimore: Johns Hopkins University Press, 2018).

it, it will go away." Yet, in almost every crisis situation, it is relatively easy to plan ahead—to identify the impacts and consequences of the underlying issue on the institution. Failing to do so will inevitably result in a reactive response that inadvertently prolongs the crisis, undermines stakeholders' confidence in leadership to effectively manage the situation, and exacerbates the impact of the issue or event on the institution. Getting ahead of a crisis situation is not impossible; it is vital. Doing so, however, requires a shared understanding of the risk among the team members required to make decisions, and a willingness to recognize that the situation could get worse.

Overly Optimistic Assessment of Capability to Manage Crisis. There is often a misplaced confidence that the leadership team or Crisis Management Team, if one is formally in place, knows what it is doing and how it will operate, no further guidance required, even though crises do not—fortunately—occur that often. Let's compare crisis response to a fire drill. Organizations will diligently conduct a fire drill every year, asking employees to walk down twenty flights of stairs to be accounted for at a predesignated meeting space. Yet, when it comes to managing complex issues or crisis events with profound and long-term implications for the organization, most organizations seem to assume that things will, somehow, just work out because "we have lots of smart people."

The key is to recognize that crisis management is a perishable skill—a skill that, without practice, will atrophy.

Challenge 3: The Risk of Groupthink and Stress on Decision-Making

Crises are inherently difficult to manage, not just because of the negative impact and range of potential impacts they may have on an organization but also because of the psychological pressure they put on decision-makers. This psychological pressure also means that our ability to make good decisions is handicapped—just at the point where it is most important that it not be.

Groupthink is often referred to as the tendency for a close-knit group to emphasize consensus at the expense of critical thinking and decision-making. In a crisis, this can degenerate into "bunker mentality," an aggravated form of groupthink in which there is inherent suspicion of all criticism. In such a dynamic, group members squash dissent, exert pressure to conform, suppress information from those who disagree, and focus selectively on information that supports the group's point of view, referred to as "confirmation bias." In such a situation, only information that conforms to the prevailing group view is sought out, accepted, and used to further strengthen the existing point of view; contrary information is discounted as being wrong.

In meetings, this tendency is made worse, as individuals are less likely to bring up new information until they understand whether it conforms to the prevailing perspective of the group. Information that is dissonant is typically not shared by an individual, even though it leads to poor decision-making. Staying silent or not sharing new information is rationalized as not being important to the decision. The final nail in the coffin is that the team is unable to self-diagnose any of the symptoms of groupthink outlined above. If this is the dynamic inside the leadership team, what hope is there to effectively diagnose the risks and its impacts, let alone effectively respond?

Research also suggests that "crisis-induced stress makes decision makers cognitively rigid. They seek premature closure, fail to search all alternatives and evaluate alternatives on one rather than all important values . . . They may view subordinates who advocate a different course of action as interference rather than a source of useful information and ideas to improve the decision."* Crises tend to make the already existing risks of groupthink on good decision-making worse.

*Alexander L. George, "The Impact of Crisis-Induced Stress on Decision Making," in *The Medical Implications of Nuclear War* (Washington, DC: National Academies Press, 1986.)

Understanding these likely team dynamics and actively try-ing to counter them in advance—for example, by actively seeking dissonant points of view, getting everyone to share their per-spective of the risk before rather than after decisions have been made—is important for the success of the crisis management ef-fort. Sometimes, institutions will seek out an outside and expe-rienced perspective to mitigate the risk of groupthink, which can lead to either (1) better risk assessment and decision-making or (2) quickly ignoring the advice from the third party when it turns out to not conform with the desired input. While there are chal-lenges associated with operating as a group, research also suggests that, while not perfect, a team approach is most effective, par-ticularly when the situation becomes more nebulous, complex, and unpredictable—like a crisis!

The Role of a Strong Leader

These challenges can easily be compounded when the president is actively and intimately engaged in the response. Rather than using the strength of the team to come up with appropriate op-tions and strategies to be presented to the president for final decision-making or agreement, with the president in the room the risk that the team will limit options to what they believe or think the president is wanting to happen or to hear is exacerbated.

It is the president's responsibility to understand the outsized influence he or she can have on the thinking of team members and actively give them space to deliberate, discuss, and openly disagree on the risks, options, and optimal strategies. The dy-namic required to fully assess the situation, get the team to share the risks and consequences of the event, and come up with some viable options is difficult to accomplish when the president is in the room. The team, rather than being a group of peers, will typ-ically defer to the wishes or assessment of the president, which may be based on an inaccurate or skewed assessment of risk.

This is perhaps the hardest thing for a president to hear, and one of the most difficult things to achieve during an actual crisis, particularly when the president may view his or her leadership to be specifically at risk. Crisis leadership is addressed in more detail in chapter 8, including the challenges inherent in being both a first-time president and a long-time leader.

Challenge 4: Reliance on Existing Leadership Structures or an Ad Hoc Response

Many universities have an Executive Policy Group, identified as part of their Emergency Management Plan, which is intended to serve as the strategic and policy-making function during an emergency. Unfortunately, this EPG is only activated during a time when the Emergency Operations Center is also activated, that is, in response to physical risks. Even for physical events, this concept is insufficient, as the strategic implications of an event like an active shooter or a building collapse can and typically does outlast an EOC activation. What is the defined process to enable sustained strategic engagement by the leadership team? These plans are also generally silent on the plethora of reputational risks on campus that need defined leadership engagement, clear risk assessment, strategy and policy-making, and coordinated stakeholder communications.

Reliance on Existing Teams

One typical suboptimal response is simply to use an existing leadership team—either the president's cabinet or senior leadership team or equivalent group. There are a number of problems with this default approach.

The process doesn't acknowledge that a crisis is NOT business as usual. Using a team that may have its own dynamic and process and, because of inevitable scheduling difficulties, might meet only once a month and is designed for another purpose, is an immediate barrier to prompt and prioritized decision-making. A crisis is not business as usual, and anything that suggests that it is will only serve to handicap the effectiveness of the response. Convening the Crisis Management Team needs to actually mean something within the organization—that things are going to be done in a different way, that the usual decision-making and approval processes are going to have to be temporarily put aside in order to meet the challenge of the day. It is a process and a mindset—and the mindset needs to change.

The team membership of the Executive Leadership Team (ELT) may not be what is required for an effective crisis response team. Depending on the organization, an existing group could be too small (three or four members) and thus not broadly representative of critical functions, thus limiting the team's ability to truly understand the potential ramifications of the crisis. Conversely, and this is more often the case, the existing ELT, with fifteen or twenty members and sometimes even more, could be too large and unwieldy to function effectively as a Crisis Management Team. This large group of senior leaders may need to be informed about the progress of the issue or crisis and what decisions are being made; typically, not all senior leaders are needed for effective response and decision-making in each specific instance. A CMT can be a subset of the ELT; again, if this decision is not purposefully thought through and agreed to before any crisis event, an effective response will be hobbled.

Ad Hoc Response by Leader Closest to Issue

Another common mistake is to decide that the leader closest to the issue should be responsible, rather than trying to solve the crisis through a defined, cross-functional team. If a functional leader is assigned to manage the crisis in their area, there is inherent risk that there will be too much confidence in the ability of their functional team, a failure to challenge assumptions, and typically a failure to understand the concerns of other stakeholders, who do not share the same level of expertise. The lack of early recognition of the potential broader impacts and consequences of the underlying event is often the recipe for the crisis to be inadequately managed and for its impact to become worse, not better, over time. "Too little, too late" is the typical outcome.

For example, if the crisis is generated by the institution's business school, the response is almost guaranteed to be poor, if responsibility for managing the issue is handed back to the dean to resolve. The dean may believe that central administration either doesn't understand the relevant facts or is exaggerating the severity of the impact of the business school issue on the institution as a whole. As will be discussed in more detail, *crisis management is not about managing the incident or event—it is about managing the impacts and consequences*—and thus by definition needs to be managed at a central administration level, not at a department or unit level.

Finally, by tasking the person with the most to do in their issue area to additionally lead the broader crisis management effort leads to the worst of both worlds: it both detracts from their operational responsibilities and also impedes their ability to properly consider the broader strategic impacts and consequences of the event on the institution. This ad hoc and inherently inconsistent approach also makes it impossible for the institution to actually build a capability to manage crises and get better at it—something that is not only possible but important to accomplish.

Challenge 5: Chaos as an Acceptable Operating Model

There are many, many other things that can and do go wrong during a crisis that are not a result of the precipitating issue or event but that are caused by insufficient preparation. Crises are difficult enough to manage without making up the response process as you go along. Getting the team into the "room" (virtual or otherwise) is critical but insufficient. Unfortunately, many plans tend to say little about how the CMT or other teams should function beyond a room location and who should show up! Too much happens too fast for the management process not to be clear or for CMT meetings to go on for hours. Chaos is not an acceptable operating model, but it is sometimes accepted in a crisis situation.

War Rooms

Some plans do not really define how the team will operate per se but identify where the team will meet and what resources a "war room" may need to have. War rooms can be extremely helpful and can coexist and support a defined management and decision-making process.

Unfortunately, in many instances, the existence of a war room replaces rather than augments a defined meeting process. Rather than aiding effectiveness, these war rooms can actually intensify some of the challenges inherent in a crisis, particularly (1) rolling meetings without end or focus; (2) multiple teams wanting to co-locate in the one room, blurring the division of labor between teams; and (3) skewing the focus of response onto the immediate, tactical elements as opposed to the broader, strategic issues the CMT needs to make sure it does not forget to anticipate.

War rooms are typically equipped with TV monitors, video-conferencing facilities, and dedicated technology, including fixed-line phones, status boards, backup power, etc. These facilities are especially beneficial if they allow response team members to have more accurate and timely information and be more sensitive to external developments. This granularity of information may not, however, be necessary or helpful for the Crisis Management Team, which is charged with longer-term, strategic decision-making.

In one instance in which a CMT had a war room for effective information sharing, a president became so preoccupied with the streaming social media feed—and in particular a serial poster called Rosie Dosie—that the social media feed had to be turned off to allow for better discussion inside the room.

Challenge 6: A "Paper CMT"

The challenge with the paper CMT is that, while a crisis management plan is down on paper, it has not been socialized or shared, and the people on the team do not know what they are expected to actually do. Sometimes—and this is particularly true if crisis management plans are developed without direct input from leadership—the team may not have any real authority at all, and the president or other leaders may create, on the fly, their own team to manage the response to the event, either not knowing that something is already in place or simply not believing that what is in place is up to the task. At other times, the CMT process may actually work fairly well, but influential members of the president's inner circle might deliberately try to circumvent the CMT, because they either (a) disagree with the consensus strategy or (b) think that strategy might lead to more discussion and divergent points of view that they view as undermining their authority.

For the board or other key stakeholders, a paper CMT is perhaps the most perilous threat because it looks as if the organization has a clear crisis management plan in place, but the plan is equal in weight and substance only to the piece of paper behind it. In this day and age, if a university's CMT isn't formerly activated at least once per year, it would be fair to assume that an informal and suboptimal process is being used to manage crises rather than that the institution has not experienced one.

Challenge 7: The Crisis Management Team Performing Another Team's Role

It can be difficult to focus on the strategic policy implications of an issue or event, particularly during the early stages of a crisis. However, if the CMT starts to perform the role of another team—such as an Emergency Response Team or the Crisis Communications

Team—the broader strategic, financial, and reputational issues are inevitably not being adequately and proactively addressed.

This unfortunately tends to happen when the leadership team does not feel that it is being appropriately briefed on the situation or does not have confidence in the ability of the subteam to do its job. All too often, a leadership team can start to make operational decisions—for example, determining how, when, and with what tools police remove protestors. This should not be a CMT decision; rather, it must focus on higher-level policy decisions vis-à-vis tolerating an occupation versus forcible removal.

Likewise, the CMT meetings can all too easily degenerate into a mass editing of proposed external media statements, time spent making "happy to glad" edits or nonsubstantive changes. While the approval of key external messaging is certainly something in which the crisis team needs to be involved, the approval process must be clear, defined, and limited. There have been instances in which the president and other senior leaders literally spent all day working on a statement only for it to be irrelevant by the time it was "finalized," so it was never actually used.

Each team should have distinct and separate responsibilities and be able to operate independently when required and operate seamlessly when response is required on multiple levels, strategically and operationally.

Challenge 8: Recognizing that Legal Strategy Is Not the Entire Strategy

Crises almost inevitably result in some type of legal risk—either due to the underlying issue or incident itself or to the failure of the institution to respond appropriately. As a result, it is important that the CMT get solid legal advice. Beyond that, the engagement of counsel, or outside counsel, is often vital to extend privilege over the internal deliberations of the team, which allows for a fuller exploration of options than would otherwise be available or which could, in hindsight, be problematic. That said, and partly because of the unique role attorneys have in a crisis—and specifically the power of extending privilege—there are a number of pitfalls that are important to avoid if the overall response is not going to be driven solely by legal considerations.

Failing to recognize that legal strategy is necessary but not sufficient for the entire institutional strategy inevitably results in a response in which the institution's reputation and leadership can be left in tatters, with only incremental benefit to the legal case. The most obvious instance of this is Michigan State University and its response to the scandal centered on Larry Nassar, a famous osteopath and doctor to the USA gymnastics squad for decades, who was convicted for molesting hundreds of gymnasts over a twenty-year period.

The initial response to criticism of sexual abuse by the doctor was to cast doubt on the veracity of the allegations and, supported by internal reports, position the incidents as misunderstood and cutting-edge medical procedures. Faced with a growing number of alleged victims, the institution doubled-down on a legal-first strategy in response to mounting legal claims. An internal investigation started by the school turned into a process to support defense counsel—as opposed to an attempt to reveal and address any failings by the institution. Finally, it wasn't until days before the president resigned that any attempt—a $10 million fund to support counseling services—was established to demonstrate contrition or support for the victims.

This legal-first strategy resulted in MSU settling a $500 million lawsuit—the biggest ever settlement in such a case against a public university. By this point, the long-standing president had resigned, soon to be followed by the athletic director, the general counsel, and a host of other leaders. The former dean of the School of Osteopathic Medicine, whom the school did not sanction for more than a year, was found guilty of multiple criminal charges, and the reputation of the institution was—just as in the Penn State and Sandusky scandals before it—indelibly damaged.

This is one of the best examples of a key premise discussed throughout this book: it is *the perception of the response that creates reputational damage,* not the underlying event. One can quite easily construct an alternate series of events in which the dean and other athletic coaches were investigated, where victims were encouraged to come forward and were provided with counseling and other support, where a commitment was made to review reporting criteria and a culture that enabled Nassar's behavior to continue for two decades, and so on. The underlying facts would have been the same, but the negative impact on the institution would have been mitigated: the willingness of victims to sue likely reduced, due to support received from the institution; and leadership credibility and authority to lead maintained.

Bifurcation of Process in Support of Privilege

One of the determinants of effective crisis response is for the team to have a shared understanding of the situation and the risks it presents. If some members of the team have incomplete information, it makes risk assessment and decision-making impossible. Sometimes "privilege" is used to effectively bifurcate the process, to divide the team into those who have a complete understanding of legal risk and those who do not.

This can be a recipe for disaster, as it essentially eviscerates the purpose of having a crisis management team in the first place. This division can sometimes occur when the legal counsel, not agreeing with or concerned about the broader strategy advocated by the team, may try to end-run the process by using both legal privilege as well as their often dual role as secretary of the board to advocate for a different strategy. None of this is typical, of course—but it needs to be watched for—and most counsel are excellent strategic advisors to the team, in addition to providing sound legal advice.

Recognizing the Difference between Legal Advice and Advice from an Attorney

Not all advice provided by an attorney is legal advice—it may be strategic advice, or it may be communications advice. All advice, experience, and perspectives are of course vital and should be welcomed—it is part of the mechanism by which teams can appropriately explore options. It is, however, important to not give more credence than necessary to the extralegal advice of general counsel or outside counsel. As such, teams should strive to have their communications not be developed by counsel in the first place, as this approach will frequently fail to resonate with the stakeholders whom it is important to influence. Likewise, edits should absolutely be considered if they bear on actual or potential litigation risk; such concerns should be properly evaluated in the context of the broader strategy.

Not Having Legal Counsel at the Table

Many smaller institutions do not have in-house legal counsel and rely, instead, on a variety of external firms to support their daily legal needs. In crisis situations, it is vital to have an attorney present to both provide a legal perspective and also, ideally, to extend legal privilege to sensitive discussions. Beyond litigation risk, public universities in particular are almost inevitably going to be subject to Freedom of Information Act (FOIA) requests or equivalent state requirements, which can be used by reporters and by nongovernmental organizations (NGOs) and activist groups to paint a highly negative picture of internal deliberations.

Challenge 9: Not Incorporating Values into Decision-Making

At the end of the day, the entire point of ensuring that challenges with group dynamics are identified and offset and that challenges associated with lack of definition of process are remedied and clear is to enable the crisis to be handled in a manner in which decisions are made in accordance with the values of the institution. Values must and should be the touchstone of the decisions being made. Failure to do so can completely destroy the trust that key stakeholders have in the leadership team. All too often, however, core institutional values take a back seat to more prosaic issues, such as legal liability, precedent setting (if we do it this time, we'll have to do it again next time), or the cost of doing something.

Sometimes, of course, there are conflicting values that make decisions even more difficult; for example, a religious institution that genuinely believes in the importance of forgiveness might lead to normally unacceptable behavior being tolerated. Another common example is the value of freedom of speech juxtaposed by the competing value of creating a welcoming and supportive climate to help students succeed, particularly first-generation, BIPOC (Black, Indigenous, and People of Color) or other underrepresented groups.

At other times, it is not the inherent complexities of the issue but the perspective different stakeholders will have regarding what "the right" response needs to be. This dynamic is particularly clear when social or political issues create a crisis on campus in which older, typically more conservative alumni are at odds with the perspective of a more liberal student body and, oftentimes, faculty. In these types of fraught situations, it is vital to distinguish between values and pressure. Just because one stakeholder group is vehemently against a particular decision does not mean that they actually represent the values of the institution.

Effectively managing response to a crisis is absolutely possible. Nobody ever said, however, that crisis management was going to be easy!

These first two chapters have articulated why reputational risk needs to be proactively managed by institutions of higher education and how poorly managed crises or unaddressed issues can have dramatic or slowly corrosive impacts on reputation. They also presented some of the common challenges to an effective response—challenges that tend to exacerbate, as opposed to mitigate, the underlying issue or event. With these issues identified, the question now becomes, What to do about it? The following chapters will address the solutions to these real problems by detailing four components of effective crisis management:

1. Issue and event reporting and escalation (Why didn't we know about this earlier?)
2. Response structure and team roles (Who else is involved and who is doing what?)
3. Defined team operations (What are we going to do?)
4. Crisis communications (What are we going to say?)

Chapter 3

Effective Crisis Management I: Getting Ahead of a Crisis

Why Didn't We Know about This Earlier?

The risk of being blindsided by events occurring on campus is considerably higher in large institutions, which may have separate hospital and clinics, multiple (including international) campuses, separate research institutions, and schools and colleges that themselves can have thousands of students and employees. While the challenge of finding out about what is going on across "campus" is inherently more complex at larger institutions, the need to have some process to escalate, assess, and then activate an appropriate and timely response is a requirement, regardless of institutional size.

Why? Because crisis management isn't just the process required to respond once an organization is in the middle of a crisis; it is a proactive approach to identify the potential impact of events early enough to *prevent* the situation from devolving into a crisis. One of the goals of effective crisis management is to prevent a serious issue or event from becoming a crisis in the first place—taking preemptive measures that both mitigate the impact of the event and demonstrate to stakeholders the seriousness with which the institution takes the issue. This ability to nip a crisis in the bud is only possible with

- clear reporting criteria and processes;
- a defined screening or analysis process to evaluate the information and put it into context with other events or issues occurring at the institution; and
- a clear escalation and team activation process.

Without these tools, "bad news" can languish unaddressed in the institution, allowing the following problems to occur:

- Information being relayed in such a way that the institution's response is not only perceived to be but actually is too slow
- Different parts of the organization having completely different understandings of information and sense of the risk, adding to confusion and internal time-wasting
- Informal, ad hoc processes being used as a stop-gap measure, because there is often no formalized response process beyond emergency management, which is focused on physical events, such as national disasters or an active shooter

The reporting and escalation process requires sensitivity to context and an ability to "connect the dots." It also defines the inflection point for the institution, when an issue or event moves from being something that can be handled by a specific unit, college, or department to something that has systemic and institution-wide impacts and consequences and requires a centralized management approach.

Issue and Event Reporting

Reporting criteria identifies a series of issues or incidents that have the potential to become a crisis if not properly managed. The reporting criteria should be tailored to reflect the unique risks to the organization, its issues management priorities, and they must be consistent across the institution—however geographically dispersed or internally fragmented. The criteria may also change over time; a school that has had a series of racially motivated issues or hazing incidents or allegations of sexual assault within athletics, for example, may rightly have a lower threshold for reporting these types of incident than an institution without that background.

The reporting criteria need to be clear and definitive yet not overly prescriptive, allowing someone to claim, "Well, it is not on the list," thus providing an excuse for not reporting. It is also important to note that these criteria are not intended to replace any existing reporting processes or chains of command, but are added to them, providing a fail-safe process by which information flows to those responsible for assessing reputational risk and assessing the required institutional response. For example, existing student conduct processes should not change, but some subset may be defined as additionally requiring reporting through a broader incident reporting process.

If the reporting bar is too low, all sorts of events will get reported that really have no potential of becoming a crisis and should, in fact, be handled at a different level in the institution.

TABLE 3.1. *Reporting Criteria: Example*

Threat of workplace violence or unusual acts that endanger students, faculty, or staff

Student or staff/faculty death that occurs off campus

Threat of protest or building occupation

IT systems failure or utility failure likely to last more than twelve hours

Sexual assault allegations implicating "high profile" individual, for example, faculty/staff/athletes

Allegations of faculty misconduct, such as plagiarism

Racial incident on campus

Hazing/inappropriate activities by fraternities or student groups

Media inquiries likely to result in sustained negative articles or unanticipated on-campus arrival of TV crews, reporters, and so on.

The reporting bar, however, should not be so high that only information about actual crises is reported. If that is the case, then the "early warning" indicator role of the reporting process will fail. As a rule of thumb, out of 100 issues or events, only about 10 percent will be of sufficient magnitude to even warrant reporting. Of that 10 percent, an even smaller percentage will warrant any action at all from the institution's Crisis Management Team.

It is vital that the reporting process be straightforward; all issues or events that meet the reporting criteria should be sent to a single place within the institution for further evaluation. This prevents the typical challenge in most organizations of different pieces of information coming in through various functional silos—legal speaking to legal, deans to the provost, communications to Communications, and so forth. Those vertical communications are inherent in any organization and will happen, whether or not there is a defined reporting and screening process.

Incident Analysis and Screening

With clarity around reporting expectations defined, and a no-fault culture in which bad news can be shared—a cultural dependency on which this process actually relies—the institution is then in a position to decide the appropriate response to receiving this initial information.

The parable of the blind men and the elephant is the easiest way to explain the value of having a defined analysis and screening process. As the story goes, each of the blind men touched a different part of the elephant—one the tail, another the tusk, a third the leg, and so on—and each drew completely different and erroneous conclusions about what they had touched: a rope, a pipe, and a tree, respectively. The purpose of the incident analysis and screening process is to metaphorically take the blinders off so that the elephant in the room can in fact be seen for what it is.

A defined reporting and screening process helps ensure that information is shared in a consistent and predictable manner and

Take Off the Blinders

subsequently analyzed by a small, cross-functional group that has a broad view of the risk and strategy of the institution. The incident analysis and screening process is the "intelligence" of the crisis management process. It takes the raw information shared through the reporting process and analyzes the potential risk this event or issue has for the institution as a whole. This analysis is formed through two lines of exploration: (1) How bad could this become?, that is, looking beyond the facts as they are currently known; and (2) What could the impact of this be?, that is, what other, seemingly unrelated issues or events could be complicated by, or become more complicated, because of this event?

How Bad Could This Become?

Andy Grove, former CEO of Intel, is famous for his saying and book of the same title, *Only the Paranoid Survive*. Individuals within organizations facing a crisis are typically overly optimistic about the chances of a good outcome or are overly confident in the ability of leaders to resolve the issue. Somewhere between paranoia and optimism sits the incident analysis and screening process. It needs to be, at a minimum, skeptical, and ideally it will challenge any assertions that "everything is being taken care of." The analysis is not intended to second-guess those who are directly working on the issue or event but rather to make some reasonable assumptions about how bad the issue could become. If the issue is concern over a potential data breach, is it reasonable to take the potentially rosy forecasts of the IT department or to consider that the breach is considerably bigger and broader than currently understood? By proactively analyzing the initial information and looking at reasonable risks, and by activating the appropriate team early on, it is possible to get ahead of the crisis rather than remain behind events.

What Else Could This Impact?

As with any crisis, it is rarely the specific issue or event that causes the crisis but the context in which the event happens. The incident analysis therefore needs to look beyond the event itself in order to understand the real risk—a Title IX complaint involving a member of faculty may not normally cause a potential crisis for an institution. However, if this is the third such report, or if there are other allegations rumbling around in Athletics, or if the institution has just been sued by an employee for sexual discrimination, it may be that this is a broader issue, one that significantly increases risk to the organization and requires a more concerted and comprehensive strategy and response concerning Title IX issues.

Beyond the campus context, it is also important to recognize the role and impact of broader societal contexts in this evaluation process—for example, the #MeToo movement in 2017 and Black Lives Matter in 2014 and 2020. This is not to suggest the underlying event is any more or less important or should not follow existing defined protocols. Rather, these examples reinforce the role of crisis management: to manage the impacts and consequences of an event, not the event itself. Societal pressures can change the potential impact and saliency of any issues that may, therefore, require more concerted leadership engagement and potentially broader changes to strategy, policy, and approach.

The analysis, therefore, needs to look not just at the specifics of the incident or issue that has been reported but also at the broader organizational and societal context in which the event is taking place. This can also include non-crisis-related events, such as Convocation, a board meeting or an upcoming Faculty

Crises Don't Happen in a Vacuum

Some of the most unbelievably inappropriate things can occur on campus if the administration is unable to connect the dots between seemingly unrelated events. Examples include:

- In the middle of student protests around tuition increases and the "corporatization" of higher education, a school was about to announce a corporate advisory board with leaders from major corporations headquartered in the area.
- Days after removing a dean for unethical conduct, the institution learned that he was going to receive an award from a different part of the school for ethical leadership.
- In the middle of a rollout plan for financial cuts, the college realized that the former president's large deferred compensation package would become public.
- The potentially deadly infection in a primate research center became public the same weekend that a new *Planet of the Apes* movie opened.
- In the middle of protests around police conduct, the institution learned that the Police Department was about to accept an offer of a free military surplus tank.

The impact of these potential issues and events was mitigated because of the institutions' screening process and ability to evaluate the risk in the broader context of events occurring on campus. The tank was never accepted, the award was never given, and the advisory board announcement was significantly postponed.

Senate meeting, all of which could potentially increase interest in and scrutiny of the administration's response.

How does this process become part of the culture and expectations at an institution? Ideally, as part of a crisis management planning process, a small cross-functional team is identified and tasked with the responsibility of promptly reviewing and analyzing any reports that are received.

Team members need to be senior enough to have a high level of visibility into broad organizational issues and have a good perspective of risk. Typical members—because of the perspective they bring to the organization—can include a senior member of communications, risk management, legal, or the offices of finance and administration (which often oversee facilities, police, etc.). Depending on the size of the organization, members can either be the vice president or a direct report to the vice president.

The incident analysis and screening process should have a minimum of three options to guide the response to the reported incident. Options may increase based on organizational complexity.

Do Nothing/Monitor. Based on the information shared and the broader assessment of risk, the decision could be made that the underlying issue or event is being appropriately and effectively managed, and that there is essentially no risk to the institution as a whole; for example, the Emergency Operations Team is handling the situation effectively, or the issue is limited to and is being handled appropriately at the college or departmental level, and there is no need for senior-level engagement.

A word of caution here. That determination needs to be made by the screening team, not the part of the institution that has the particular issue and has made the initial report. If an event meets the reporting criteria, it is the screening team that has the authority to determine the need to engage other parts of the organization in the response, not the team where the incident occurred; that team will likely be defensive in such circumstances, and it doesn't have the broader context to make the appropriate determination.

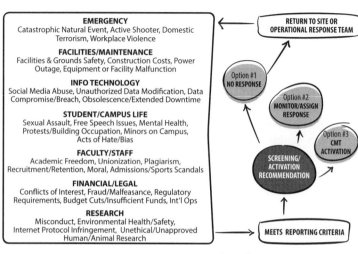

EMERGENCY
Catastrophic Natural Event, Active Shooter, Domestic Terrorism, Workplace Violence

FACILITIES/MAINTENANCE
Facilities & Grounds Safety, Construction Costs, Power Outage, Equipment or Facility Malfunction

INFO TECHNOLOGY
Social Media Abuse, Unauthorized Data Modification, Data Compromise/Breach, Obsolescence/Extended Downtime

STUDENT/CAMPUS LIFE
Sexual Assault, Free Speech Issues, Mental Health, Protests/Building Occupation, Minors on Campus, Acts of Hate/Bias

FACULTY/STAFF
Academic Freedom, Unionization, Plagiarism, Recruitment/Retention, Moral, Admissions/Sports Scandals

FINANCIAL/LEGAL
Conflicts of Interest, Fraud/Malfeasance, Regulatory Requirements, Budget Cuts/Insufficient Funds, Int'l Ops

RESEARCH
Misconduct, Environmental Health/Safety, Internet Protocol Infringement, Unethical/Unapproved Human/Animal Research

RETURN TO SITE OR OPERATIONAL RESPONSE TEAM

Option #1 NO RESPONSE

Option #2 MONITOR/ASSIGN RESPONSE

Option #3 CMT ACTIVATION

SCREENING/ ACTIVATION RECOMMENDATION

MEETS REPORTING CRITERIA

Issue or Event Reporting and Escalation

In cases when no additional engagement is viewed as necessary, there will typically be a request for further updates should the situation deteriorate and a different level of response be required.

Assign Responsibility or Provide Additional Resources. While the assessment may suggest that there is little to no risk to the institution as a whole, there may be additional support or guidance, which could speed up the response. This could take the form of specific expertise that exists externally or in a different part of the institution; it could be procurement of additional supplies or reallocation of resources from one part of the institution to another; it could be identifying appropriate outside legal counsel to provide guidance, and so forth. Whatever the specific nature of the support that might be helpful, this support would be coordinated—if it is not already—through the usual reporting channels. The role of the screening team in this instance is simply to assure broader awareness of the issue and make sure that any specific expertise or resource is made available.

In some large institutions, there may be another interim option available: activating an Incident Response Team or risk-specific teams that already exist. The assessment of the situation does not require senior-level active engagement or decision-making, but it would benefit from a cross-functional team to carefully monitor and manage response to an incident or issue. An example might be a Data Breach Response Team (which needs to be broader than IT, for example) or more recently, a COVID-19 Response Team. Earlier, we defined a crisis as requiring a threat, urgency, and uncertainty. In situations when there is no uncertainty, but instead a need to execute pre-agreed-upon plans and responses, the Crisis Management Team will usually not be necessary. In small colleges, obviously, this kind of multilevel response is not possible, or in fact needed, and the threshold for convening the CMT is going to be considerably lower than in a larger institution.

Convene the Crisis Management Team. Owing to the potential for the underlying issue or event to become significantly worse, and because of the potential for a significant institutional impact, the screening group makes the decision to bring the CMT together for a full briefing about the issue or event. At this meeting, the team will determine if it is going to fully activate as the team responsible for the overall management of the issue (wherever normal day-to-day responsibility may lie), or whether it would be more appropriately managed by a smaller working group or an already established team.

Implementing Challenges

There are two challenges to this part of this process. The first is prioritizing this analysis and screening activity. If the information is reported promptly but then not looked at for days because of scheduling conflicts and other priorities, it will not work. Members of the screening group—which needs to be clearly defined—must make this assessment process a priority. It should

only take between ten and fifteen minutes for this group to review the information, consider what else is going on, and how
bad it could become to inform their decision about the appropriate next step.

The second challenge is an unwillingness to actively consider
worst probable scenarios for fear of undermining their own
credibility within the organization (being perceived as crying
wolf) if the worst probable does not materialize. Both of these
legitimate concerns can eviscerate the value of the assessment
and screening process. Experience and time should overcome
these natural barriers to effective implementation. While there
may be a sense that this is taking a lot of time, it typically takes
considerably less internal time than informal and ad hoc hall-
way conversations, which also don't help ensure a timely, coordinated, and consistent level of response.

One final note. This screening and evaluation process is not
intended to be employed when it is absolutely obvious to everyone that the institution is facing a potential crisis, such as a ter-
rorist on campus, a cyberattack that shuts down systems, and
the like. In those rare events—when typically the Emergency
Management Team is also activated—it is appropriate to assume
activation is required. The process defined above, however, is
designed to provide a rigorous, consistent, and predictable process for the usually vast "grey area" between an incident and a
crisis—for when it is not obvious at all.

Putting this reporting process in place helps ensure that there is
a broad view and an understanding of what is happening throughout the institution, an analysis and screening function that can review information and connect the dots to assess the potential risk
to the organization, and a clear process to convene the Crisis Management Team. This solves the "Why didn't we learn about this
earlier?" challenge common to most self-inflicted crises. The vital
next step, as discussed in chapter 4, is to ensure that there is clarity
in the roles and responsibilities of the CMT and how it will coordinate and align with others across the organization.

Effective Crisis Management II: Defining Roles and Responsibilities

----

Who Else Is Involved and Who Is Doing What?

Earlier, crisis management was defined as a proactive senior-level management process that allows an organization to make fast, coordinated decisions that can withstand intense external scrutiny. While the Crisis Management Team is responsible for strategic decision-making, that is obviously not the only thing that needs to happen in a crisis. Defining the response structure—perhaps an off-putting term, but essentially defining the roles and responsibilities across the institution—means defining other areas of response and ensuring that they are aligned, coordinated, and mutually supportive. The structure needs to clarify which team or teams are responsible for doing what, how they will coordinate, how information will be shared, and how they can each effectively focus on their primary responsibilities.

The purpose of defining the response structure and team roles is to prevent the following problems from occurring:

- Lack of coordination across the organization—the proverbial left hand not knowing what the right hand is doing
- Duplication of effort caused by lack of clear divisions of labor and internal confusion over who is responsible for what
- Damage caused by the perception of the institution's not being prepared
- Decisions either being made prematurely or not being made at all

While for some small organizations the response structure may be straightforward, for many, the number of other teams could be quite broad, depending on the size and scope of the organization. It is likely to include:

- An Emergency Operations Team, and potentially site-specific emergency response teams
- Leadership teams at affiliated healthcare organizations or research facilities
- A crisis communications team to coordinate all aspects of communications across all stakeholders
- Risk-specific incident response teams, such as a data breach or privacy response team

Unfortunately, in higher education generally, even at small colleges, where organizational scale and complexity is not a justification for lack of clarity, there is a misunderstanding or lack of acknowledgment of the distinction between emergency management and crisis management. To define an appropriate response structure, it is vital that there is a clear understanding of the differences between these two important parts of every school's ability to manage crises.

Emergency Management Doesn't Equal Crisis Management

Most campuses are like small towns, with their own police, and sometimes, fire departments. Police chiefs are trained on the Incident Command System (ICS), and compliance with the National Incident Management System (NIMS) is a federal requirement for Department of Homeland Security funding. Established in 2004 by presidential directive and building on the ICS protocols developed in 1970 by California, in the aftermath of a devastating fire, the NIMS's disciplined approach to emergency management was designed primarily to solve problems of coordination and command among first responders.

Over the past ten to twenty years and particularly after the Virginia Tech shooting in 2007, a significant effort has been made to embed ICS- and NIMS-compliant emergency management procedures at campuses across the country. As a result, most universities are better prepared for on-site events such as an active shooter or a natural disaster. While important, this focus on emergency management has unfortunately given universities a false sense that they have a "crisis management" capability in place—when in fact they do not.

Emergency management plans typically focus on operational issues, which is completely appropriate and necessary. The role of leadership and executive decision-making, however, is frequently marginalized or ignored in these plans. Many allude to the role of the Executive Policy Group as the policy-making body during an emergency, but often the only role this group has is to formally "declare" a disaster. While no doubt in some extreme circumstances this may be important, this public-sector model is simply not as robust with regard to the leadership function as it needs to be—even in response to physical events.

Another critical distinction is that in most "emergency management" type events, the institution is also a "victim" of the event—a natural disaster impacting operations or an active shooter threatening the safety of everyone on campus. It is critical to understand, however, that most crises in higher education are something altogether different. They are the self-inflicted crises—academic scandal, sexual assault, and a range of financial, social, and ethical issues. The risk to institutions of higher education lies in the management of these crises, the ones that are not addressed at all by an institution's emergency management plan.

A final difference is the operating model for emergency management versus crisis management. In an emergency, the Emergency Operations Center is opened and the various subteams are activated; typically, the process is run and managed by someone in the public safety or police department of the school. The EOC may remain activated for a few hours—or in a some cases, such as a hurricane or an earthquake, in which recovery efforts need to be managed and coordinated—for a period of days. In contrast, a Crisis Management Team may be activated for weeks or months after the precipitating event to manage not just the event but its aftermath.

All of these are substantive differences in role, range of risks, and operating model. Understanding the critical role of crisis management in effective decision-making and response is undermined, unfortunately, by a tendency to conflate crisis communications with crisis management. These hands-on responders tend to reduce everything else the institution has to do to being about "communications," oftentimes failing to recognize that effective communications requires substantive policy- and decision-making in order to be credible.

One of the clearest ways to describe the difference between an EMT and a CMT is that the EMT is operational and is "looking down," and the CMT is strategic and is "looking out"; in other words, starting to anticipate the knock-on impacts and consequences of the underlying event. COVID-19 has, or at least should have, exposed clearly the significant differences between operational and strategic priorities.

Defining Roles in Protest Management

Another area in which there is potential for confusion in roles is in protest management, which, when it goes wrong, can create

TABLE 4.1. *Operational vs. Strategic Priorities—COVID-19*

COVID-19: EMT/Operational Priorities	COVID-19: CMT/Strategic Priorities
Room capacities, layout, and technology	Decision on in-person or virtual operations
Classroom scheduling	Identification of shutdown or reopen thresholds
Housing options	Forecasting and decision-making regarding offsets to potential financial impacts and consequences
Food service options	
Transportation	
Staff/faculty/student safety	
Work-from-home and technology solutions	
Testing protocols	Policies related to complaints and litigation related to fees and tuition
Vaccine protocols	Racial/social equity issues related to COVID-19

long-standing and potentially unrecoverable damage to the reputation of the institution and its leadership. Since the birth of the Free Speech Movement at UC Berkeley in the 1960s, colleges and universities have highlighted the critical nature of free expression as fundamental to their mission. The ability of universities to both enable and support peaceful protest while protecting people and property has been a fundamental challenge ever since.

The Kent State Massacre in 1970, in which National Guard troops shot and killed four students and injured nine others, after days of unrest and vandalism both on campus and in the town, is the most infamous example and represents a broader, societal breakdown. It is but one example of how enforcement actions by the police, or in this case the National Guard, typically increase the radicalization of protestors, increase media interest, and exacerbate tensions, which is why de-escalation is a primary goal of protest management. Kent State does make more recent protests—whether driven by the Occupy Wall Street movement in the early 2010s, or more recent white supremacy-inspired protests seem almost peaceful. The only time the National Guard has ever been on a campus since has been in response to natural disasters.

A far more benign incident at UC Davis, in which protestors were pepper-sprayed as they were sitting on the ground blocking a pathway and refusing to move, spawned multiple litigation, multiple internal and third-party reviews, and a complete reconsideration of the role of the police and the role of the administration in protest management, as described in detail in the Robinson Edley Report.* The chief of police resigned, as did the chancellor, many years later but still in direct response to the event.

One of the central points of the Robinson Edley Report and aligned to the primary purpose of this chapter is the need to have clearly defined roles and responsibilities among the campus police, emergency management, and the university administration leadership in a fast-evolving protest situation. This applies whether the event has been approved and scheduled; is a spontaneous act of civil disobedience, including building takeovers and sit-ins; or shouting down or preventing speakers from delivering their remarks.

As in the table pertaining to COVID-19, the next table illustrates a simplified distinction between operational and strategic priorities in protest management. All of this assumes that the dynamic is essentially stable and that there is time to formulate an appropriate response, as opposed to the situation in a riot, for example.

An Institution's Response Structure

Each team, each component in the response structure, should have a distinct and defined role, different from the role of any other team. The primary challenge to appropriately align the roles and responsibilities of different teams is the limited and functionally siloed view of what is required. Institutions typically develop

*See https://campusprotestreport.universityofcalifornia.edu/.

TABLE 4.2. *Operational vs. Strategic Priorities—Protest Management*

Protest: EMT (Police)/Operational Priorities	Protest: CMT/Strategic Priorities
Protection/lockdown of critical spaces (labs, power plant)	Decision to postpone or cancel previously approved event due to security concerns
Alerts/notifications to campus community	Identify impacts and consequences of options available in advance of decisions being made on, for example, First Amendment rights, litigation, reputational damage
Coordinated approach with Student Affairs and Public Safety to support de-escalation	
Operational decisions on how to most safely achieve strategic objective defined by CMT	Decision to allow or prevent acts of civil disobedience from continuing, including decision for police to start to arrest protestors
Coordination with outside law enforcement, if/as required for public safety	Decision on variances on normal student/faculty disciplinary procedures
	Stakeholder communications

different plans over time and, with diffuse ownership, fail to recognize—at least in a consistent way—the point at which the management for that type of specific issue or event has broader impacts and consequences and would require engagement by the CMT. This is particularly true in higher education, when Facilities, Public Safety, and others often mistakenly believe that the Emergency Operations plan is the only response required.

Where there is potential confusion or perceived crossover in responsibility, these areas should be clarified in advance, without the pressure exerted by a crisis event. If there is duplication, responsibility needs to be assigned. And where there is nothing in place at all, plans and teams need to be put in place. Thinking about these issues in advance will greatly ease response during a crisis and prevent many of the unforced errors that plague institutions and exacerbate reputational risk.

The crisis management plan should align with and coordinate all other aspects of the institution's response, which are important but distinct from crisis management. If it does not, the response will be uncoordinated and the perception of not being organized will damage the reputation of the institution and the credibility of its leadership team. In addition to defining this overall response structure, the unique and distinct roles and responsibilities of the Crisis Management Team itself need to be clearly defined.

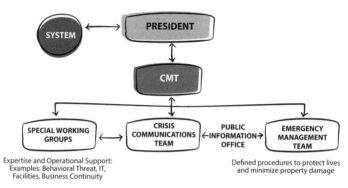

Crisis Management Response Structure

Crisis Management Team Roles and Responsibilities

The examples above are intended to make the distinction between emergency management and crisis management clear. In summary, when activated, the CMT is responsible for and has the authority to

- make policy and strategic decisions related to both reputational and physical crises that have significant implications for the institution;
- identify/forecast/manage key issues and consequences stemming from the incident or issue;
- provide strategic guidance to the Emergency Management Team when it is activated and serving as its Executive Policy Group in those instances; and

Response Structure in Systems

Defining the appropriate response structure at each institution is vital. It is even more important when a school is just one campus in a larger system—such as the University of California system or the State University of New York (SUNY), or private institutions with multiple campuses. These systems are very different—some are very top-down, others are highly decentralized, with a great deal of autonomy given to associated schools. Whatever the statutory requirements, cultural precedents, and informal expectations, the roles and responsibilities of specific schools in a system must be defined in advance of a crisis.

What is a "system" issue, which requires leadership by the overarching administration of the system? What is a "campus" issue, which can be managed by the leadership team in place at a specific location and has little to no system-wide impacts or consequences? Beyond defining the issues, it is important to establish

- clear reporting and escalation criteria between campus and system;
- clear information sharing and coordination procedures, so the campus and system offices have a shared sense of the risks and related strategies;
- clear alignment of decision-making toward commonly agreed objectives; and
- consistent communications to all stakeholders from different parts of the broader organization.

The challenge in a crisis situation is that if the campus and system office are not used to working together, under significant pressure and time constraints, lack of clarity over roles can very quickly lead to an uncoordinated and disjointed response—further impacting the reputation of the specific institution and, potentially, the system as a whole.

- approve the communications strategy and key messages developed by the Crisis Communications Team for both internal and external stakeholders.

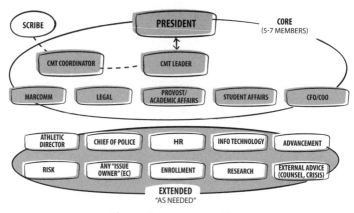

SCRIBE

PRESIDENT

CORE
(5-7 MEMBERS)

CMT COORDINATOR

CMT LEADER

MARCOMM LEGAL PROVOST/ACADEMIC AFFAIRS STUDENT AFFAIRS CFO/COO

ATHLETIC DIRECTOR CHIEF OF POLICE HR INFO TECHNOLOGY ADVANCEMENT

RISK ANY "ISSUE OWNER" (EC) ENROLLMENT RESEARCH EXTERNAL ADVICE (COUNSEL, CRISIS)

EXTENDED
"AS NEEDED"

The Crisis Management Team

Understanding the CMT's roles can help inform thinking around its membership. Another prism through which to look to decide who needs to be on the team is to recognize who is particularly attuned to the needs and concerns of the stakeholders most affected by the crisis. The team should not grow larger than six to eight members or it will become too cumbersome and slow. While each institution is different, core members—in other words, roles that are engaged in response to every type of crisis situation—usually include the vice presidents of Business/Administration, Marketing/Communications, and Student Affairs, as well as the provost, and the general counsel.

Having a defined and consistent core membership of the CMT has a number of important advantages:

- It prevents needless delays caused by bringing a group together in an ad hoc and piecemeal way, based on the perceived risk to the institution by one part of the institution

- It allows the team to coalesce as a group, to learn from previous mistakes, and simply get better at managing significant events or issues
- It makes it possible to use a defined, consistent management process that should reduce mistakes, reduce risk and increase predictability of response

Having a core team does not preclude the addition of other team members if the specifics of the event warrant it and where expertise is required. Extended team members would be brought in depending on the particular crisis and could include the vice presidents of Alumni Affairs and of Research, the athletic director, specific deans, the chief information officer, the CEO of the Hospital, the chief investment officer for schools with a significant endowment to manage, and so on. Even though some of these leaders will not be engaged for every Crisis Management Team activation, the general consistency in membership will help with consistency in management process. This is further helped by the selection of three other important roles that need to be defined and agreed.

The CMT Leader. This book discusses the role of the president in crisis in more detail in chapter 8, and specifically the relationship between the CMT leader and the president. In summary, however, the CMT leader should *not* be the president, for many of the reasons outlined in chapter 2. Rather, the leader should be a chief lieutenant, the exact role depending on the institution. Three roles are typical: the vice present for Business and Administration, the general counsel, and sometimes, depending on the authority of the person, the chief of staff to the president.

The role of the CMT leader is to run the CMT and to have specific authority to respond to the issue or event, excepting those policy or strategic decisions specifically identified and reserved for decision-making by the president or potentially the board, depending on the situation. While the president may participate in CMT meeting frequently during the early stages of a crisis, it is important that the CMT meeting process be able to continue whether or not the President is available—either due to non-crisis-related priorities or to the President's inevitably having an important, strategic role in communicating with key stakeholders, the board etc.

The CMT Coordinator. Akin to a chief of staff, the CMT coordinator supports the CMT leader, coordinates activities and progress between formal meetings, and helps ensure a high level of participation from those who are meant to be part of the CMT process. The coordinator must also interact with all other activated response teams as well as serve as a point person, briefing other leaders not directly engaged in the response. Exactly who should play this role also depends on the organization and can include the president's chief of staff (again, depending on how that is defined).

The Scribe. While attending all meetings, this role is not assigned to a member of the CMT per se but to a trusted and capable executive assistant with responsibilities to memorialize the discussions, support the CMT coordinator by sharing information with the team on action items and decisions made (discussed in greater detail in chapter 5), and broadly support administrative duties, such as scheduling meetings and so on.

Crisis Management Team Authority

For the team to function properly in the stressful environment it is in, however, each member must be able to represent that function and make decisions for it in the context of the CMT activation, even when that authority is not there in a normal operating environment. Each member has authority because of their role on the team—not because of their normal title. This is completely different from business as usual—but a crisis, by definition, is not business as usual, and so some of our assumptions about how to effectively operate also need to change.

Sometimes it is simply not possible to get all the primary members of the CMT together, virtually or otherwise, at the same time—in the best of times, this could be due to travel or unavoidable conflicts, and in the worst case leaders may be directly impacted, for example, if the cause of the crisis is a natural disaster. Regardless of reason, the decision-making process needs to be able to continue, and the team needs to have the authority to act.

Backup team members must be appointed, as in almost all instances it is highly unlikely that every primary member will be available. It is important for backup team members who take the role of the primary member to operate with the same level of authority as the primary member. This is often a major stumbling block for organizations, as backups are almost always junior to the person they have replaced. Group dynamics, discussed earlier, tend to compound the problem of having backups fill the role of the senior leaders they are replacing.

More broadly, the team—as a team—needs to have clearly defined authority to make decisions on behalf of the institution in response to the specific issue or event. It should have that authority not because of the authority of the individuals who are identified as primary members of the team but because the team, when activated, is specifically conferred with that authority. Failing to codify that and align it with any succession planning and "disaster declaration" authority that may be addressed in an emergency management plan is essential—or just when prompt and decisive decision-making is required, the institution's capability to do so will be eviscerated.

Chapter 5

Effective Crisis Management III: From Chaos to Managed Process

----

There cannot be a crisis next week. My schedule is already full.

—Henry Kissinger

What Are We Going to Do?

A crisis, by definition, is not business as usual. It requires a distinct, defined, consistent, and repeatable management process to give the Crisis Management Team every opportunity to succeed in *managing* the crisis. Getting a team into a room is not enough; it requires specific steps:

- A consistent meeting process to help ensure information sharing and coordination
- A method to proactively identify potential impacts and consequences of the event
- Agreement about how strategies are decided, what actions are required, and how to ensure accountability and follow-through

- A process for making the best possible decision when only presented with bad options
- "Close-out" procedures, including when the crisis is over and how to capture "lessons learned" to improve capability for the next time

One way to try and understand the need for a distinct and defined crisis management process is to understand the increased speed of decision-making required during a crisis compared to a typical board meeting process. It may take several months for an agenda item to be scheduled for a board meeting—materials, background, financial projections, presentations, etc.—all due three or four weeks before the presentation itself in order to allow for sufficient review, all of which takes considerable internal resources and time. Depending on the size of the organization and its culture, a similarly long lead-time is required for issues or decisions to be scheduled for a decision by the cabinet. During a crisis, the CMT may have to make two or three substantive decisions a day, of equal significance (if not more) to the decisions that would normally have taken up to three months to gestate internally in the usual process, that is, approximately 100 times faster than the status quo.

All of this is to make the case that because a crisis is substantively a different operating environment from day to day, a crisis management plan needs to define a different operating model. Relying on business-as-usual teams or processes is simply too slow to enable an effective crisis response.

The purpose of defining Crisis Management Team operations is to prevent particular problems from occurring, which are typical in a suboptimal crisis management response.

Team members having an incomplete understanding of the situation. Lack of effective, internal information-sharing typically leads to internal confusion, duplication of effort, and in its worst form, one part of the organization doing something that is counter to the overall response. In colloquial terms, the left hand doesn't know what the right hand is doing.

Team meetings that last for hours. Undefined meetings of indeterminate length waste time, lead to team members "ducking out" to take phone calls, creating information gaps and needless repetition of basic information. Institutions of higher education are particularly prone to this problem.

Team meetings that do not end with decisions or where there is confusion about whether or not decisions have been made. A CMT is not a debating society—the team needs to agree on the risk and decisions must be made.

Team meetings that are too focused on the specifics of the incident, too tactical or operational. A crisis is created by a specific incident or issue, but the impacts and consequences are typically far broader. Teams that are not addressing broader strategic impacts and consequences are missing the forest for the trees. Response is likely to be perceived as reactive or incomplete—because it probably is—which will exacerbate the risk to the organization.

Many, many other things can, and do, go wrong, during a crisis that are not a result of the precipitating issue or event but are caused by insufficient preparation. Crises are difficult enough to manage without making up the response process as you go along—and as has already been discussed, it is the perception of the institution's response to the issue or incident, not the issue or incident itself, that causes the reputational damage.

To solve these completely solvable challenges, the crisis management plan needs to clearly define how the team will operate and make sure that those who are part of the team understand this dynamic and what is expected of them. And while the focus here is on developing a crisis plan, the plan is not the end goal. Nor is it a series of checklists; crisis management, because of its inherent uncertainty and complexity, doesn't naturally lend itself to a checklist-driven process. Rather, the goal is to develop a consistent and understood capability in an organization, the "plan" merely being the document that defines expectations and is useful for training, awareness, and continual improvement.

This is an important point: the goal should not be to have a piece of paper with the words *Crisis Management Plan* on it. As President Eisenhower is famous for saying, "A plan is useless; planning is indispensable." Or more recently, an equally appropriate quote from former heavyweight boxer Mike Tyson: "Everybody has a plan until they get punched in the mouth." What, then, needs to be in the plan? What does the process need to look like? Simplicity in approach is important during a crisis, as the situation provides quite enough complexity and challenges without the management process itself making it even more difficult. The process needs to provide sufficient time and bandwidth to allow the CMT, first, to identify the potential impacts of the incident or issue for which it must prepare, and second, to focus on the strategic issues on which it must decide. Unfortunately, organizations all too often throw any internal meeting discipline out the window when they are in a crisis.

Moving from "Chaos" to a Managed Process

Too much happens too fast for a Crisis Management Team meeting to go on for hours. Instead, they should follow a meet-break-meet cadence, with each meeting being scheduled, succinct, and focused. There are some basic ground rules to ensure that the meeting process can meet the demands of the situation and that turn the crisis from chaos to a managed process.

Situation Update. The first part of every meeting is a situation update, so that everyone is on the same page since the last meeting. A situation can change rapidly, and in crisis situations it is common not to have all the information you want or need. There is no excuse, however, for a team not being uniformly aware of what information is available to them to guide their approach and decision-making. If another team has been activated—for example, the Emergency Operations Team—the first order of business is to get the latest facts and developments from the leader of the team most closely engaged with the facts on the ground. This leader will likely stay throughout the CMT meeting—assuming it is scheduled, succinct, and focused—in order to both provide information as well as receive guidance and input from the CMT so that his or her team is then in place to execute.

Impacts and Consequences. The second part of the meeting should not be about the specific event or issue but its actual and perceived impacts and consequences. This requires other team members to share information they have received from stake-holders (influential alumni, faculty, local officials, board members, media), as well as their perspective on what the institution should begin to anticipate. It is the role of the CMT leader to keep this information-sharing focused and pertinent, but information-sharing must occur. In most cases, it is the impacts and consequences of the event that are as important, and often-times more so, than the underlying event.

Progress Report. The third part of the meeting should be an update on the defined actions that have been agreed to by the team as needing to be resolved at the current meeting. A simple Word or Excel document is all that is required to assign priority, detail of the task, responsibility, and expected completion time. Google Docs are also fine as long as ownership resides with the CMT coordinator, and the meeting does not degenerate into a free-for-all. This part of the meeting should be fairly succinct and helps ensure that progress is being made on agreed action items and if problems are developing that there is awareness among team members.

Strategic Discussion. The fourth part of the meeting should be a discussion of one, at the most two, strategic issues that have been tabled for consideration. It is simply impossible in one meeting to address and agree to all strategic issues that will be raised by the issue or event. Nevertheless, recommendations must be made and agreed on. When a strategic decision has been made, it is likely that it will lead to a further series of action items, which will need to be completed to execute the strategy. For example, if a decision is made to launch an independent inquiry into what happened, it is important to define the process to identify a qualified and credible firm, to establish a clear time-line, to decide whether the report will be public or confidential, and to develop an appropriate communications strategy to inform key stakeholders of the decision.

Recap and Next Steps. The final part of the meeting should be to recap new action items and decisions that have been made so that everyone understands what the team has decided. The next meeting, if not already scheduled, needs to be scheduled at a time that meets response requirements and the tempo of the event. Teams may meet three times a day or more during the early stages of a crisis before settling into either once or twice a day, and as the issue focuses more on longer-term impacts and institutional recovery, potentially once or twice a week. Most importantly, regardless of frequency of meetings, the same discipline, focus, and commitment must be made by all members of the CMT until the team is formally deactivated.

This may seem like a lot to do and certainly in some of the initial meetings, when there is so much up in the air and the team hasn't coalesced into a pattern, it will be difficult. It is particularly hard if the team is new, or it is the first time they have had to respond to an actual crisis. However, as the team gets used to a rigorous process and as the capability of the team grows, there will be an expectation—because of the pressure of events and issues—that the CMT meetings be run in this kind of focused, efficient, and predictable manner. And this is just what needs to happen during meetings!

In-between Meetings. The vast majority of the response effort is going to happen outside these defined meetings. Action items need to be completed. Team members may need to meet with others in their department to debrief them or assign certain tasks that need to be completed. Unrelated work may need to be

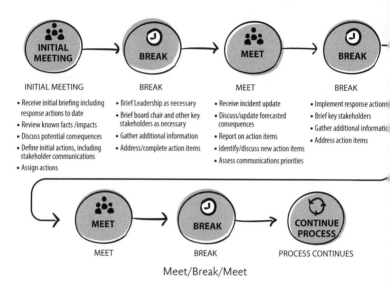

INITIAL MEETING	BREAK	MEET	BREAK
• Receive initial briefing including response actions to date • Review known facts /impacts • Discuss potential consequences • Define initial actions, including stakeholder communications • Assign actions	• Brief Leadership as necessary • Brief board chair and other key stakeholders as necessary • Gather additional information • Address/complete action items	• Receive incident update • Discuss/update forecasted consequences • Report on action items • Identify/discuss new action items • Assess communications priorities	• Implement response actions • Brief key stakeholders • Gather additional informatic • Address action items

MEET	BREAK	PROCESS CONTINUES

Meet/Break/Meet

reassigned and previous priorities postponed or moved forward in a different way. The CMT leader may need to brief others in the organization; the president and the CMT leader may need to brief the board chair or the Executive Committee, or potentially the full board. The CMT coordinator will need to follow up with specific team members on identified action items, help identify additional resources, and develop the defined agenda (together with the CMT leader) for the next CMT meeting.

Proactive Identification of Impacts and Consequences

Amid all the activity occurring during and between CMT meetings, as well as all the various stakeholder enquiries and external developments that will inevitably arise during the crisis event, it is very hard—without a conscious effort—for the team to start to look ahead at what else may be heading its way. In fact, sometimes there is a high level of reluctance to discuss what else could do wrong, what else the organization needs to be thinking about. That tendency is quite understandable, but it is counterproductive and will likely end up adding to the stress and work that needs to be done.

In almost every crisis or issue, there is a series of fairly predictable knock-on impacts that will happen. In a data breach, for example, the initial estimate of the number of impacted individuals is typically too low, and over time is recalibrated upward, sometimes by huge numbers; information is discovered about patches that weren't updated or security warnings that were not heeded; social media and traditional media will start to drag up unrelated stories about perceived past management failures; questions will be raised about financial priorities, training, security policies, etc.; litigation will be threatened or filed by former employees, customers, etc. These are all highly predictable impacts of the initial event. There is a similar pattern in almost all crises, whether a budgetary challenge requiring the announcement of program closures, a protest or occupation of the president's office, allegations of ignored sexual assault, a workplace violence event, and so on.

Given the relative predictability of likely impacts and consequences stemming from a crisis, with some effort it is possible to begin to get into a more proactive decision-making mode. Organizations that are good at crisis management start immediately to think beyond the event to understand its impact. A conscious attempt to understand and record those likely impacts can help not only identify potential risk but also help get the team on the same page in terms of what problem they are really trying to solve for. Decisions made in a crisis often look poor with the 20/20 hindsight that post-event analysis brings. But through consciously trying to identify potential impacts, likely consequences, stakeholder expectations, as well as making some reasonable

Defining a Planning Case

One of the challenges faced in almost every crisis is the lack of a shared perspective by members of the CMT on the scope and impact of the crisis. Inevitably, some members believe that the worst of the situation is behind the institution; others, that the sky is about to fall. Without a shared agreement about what the risks actually are, it should not be surprising that it is often difficult to reach a consensus on what the appropriate response should be.

A planning case is used to create a shared understanding, not of what has already happened, but what the institution needs to be prepared for. It defines a conceivable "worst *probable* outcome," which helps the CMT move beyond a "react-respond" mode to thinking ahead to identify decisions that need to be taken proactively to reduce anticipated operational, financial, legal, and reputational impacts. Layering on top a stakeholder-specific approach can help ensure that the organization's response is proactive.

Let's take as an example the Thirty Meter Telescope, or TMT, a joint enterprise of Caltech, the University of California, and various international governments, to build a next-generation telescope on the top of Mount Mauna Kea on the Big Island of Hawaii, the best location for telescopes in the Northern Hemisphere but also a sacred site for native Hawaiians.

There were plenty of warning signs that building on this site would be problematic—a ceremonial groundbreaking was interrupted a number of months before any actual construction was scheduled to begin. As construction day neared, protestors gathered—including children with leis and elders in ceremonial outfits. Construction could not start, some protestors were arrested for trespassing and blocking a road, and the number of protestors grew. Legal challenges were filed, the Hawaii Supreme Court intervened, and Hollywood stars joined the protest. You know you have problems when you are on the opposite side of Dwayne Johnson ("the Rock"), Jason Mamoa (Aquaman), and Mark Ruffalo (the Incredible Hulk)!

All of this was quite foreseeable—indeed, arguably highly likely, which brings us back to the concept of a planning case. If TMT engaged in any kind of planning case is not clear from publicly available information. Regardless, the primary strategy—to rely on the project's narrow legal "right to build" as sufficient, rather than on a more comprehensive and sustained effort of community relations and advocacy—never seemed to waver. The delays caused by the protests led to the estimated cost of the TMT project increasing from $1.4 billion to $2 billion. This was certainly predictable, and the projected increase in costs alone should have suggested that some of that $600 million would have been better used on an effort to build community support and understanding.

Whether or not TMT will ever be built in Hawaii—or even started—is currently an unknown. Its reputation, however, has now led to similar problems in its plan B site, in the Canary Islands.

assumptions about how understanding of the event is likely to change over time—to define a *worst probable* case—the team can "future-proof" the decisions it is making.

The typical phrase used to describe an organization's poor crisis response is "too little, too late" or being "caught behind the eight ball." Just as lack of organization is not inevitable in a crisis, being reactive rather than proactive is also not unavoidable. The issue or event almost always moves away from the specifics of what happened to how effective the response was. As bears repeating, the perception of the effectiveness of the response is the largest determining factor in the impact of the event on the reputation of the organization and how quickly, if ever, it recovers from the crisis.

Caught between a Rock and a Hard Place: Making Difficult Decisions

Even with a managed process in place, as well as a conscious effort to proactively identify and then start to manage impacts and consequences stemming from the underlying issue or event, the team is still going to be faced with some very difficult decisions—decisions that juxtapose two bad options or decisions, each of which creates a series of negative impacts or decisions that potentially place stakeholder groups against one another.

Instinct and intuition can only get you so far. Values can often be contradictory or at odds with each other. At the end of the day, a value judgment will have to be made, but having a consistent methodology to assess viable, albeit problematic, options can help the team reach consensus. We also believe that when facing hard decisions, "eyes wide open" is far more important than comfortable deniability by not consciously anticipating what could happen next.

To achieve this, an options analysis tool can help the team consistently assess the risks, benefits, dependencies, and resulting messaging regarding challenging decisions the team is deliberating. To begin, we recommend the team define the options and provide a shorthand name for each possible approach, for example, "Stay the Course" versus "He's Got to Go" or other suitably pithy shorthand descriptors. They should then address the following for each:

- *Benefits:* the benefits associated with the approach—ideally, distinct benefits as opposed to the simple absence of risk.
- *Risks:* the range of risks associated with the option, not just to help inform the right decision but to head off individuals who might want to second-guess the decision made as the crisis evolves. By defining in advance the risk of litigation, for example, being sued later shouldn't be viewed as a surprise or something that could lead the institution to reverse course; the risk was anticipated and factored into the decision at the outset.
- *Dependencies:* specific action items that need to be taken or basic requirements for the proposed approach to be successful, for example, "The board remains supportive," or "We

have a strong replacement candidate." If the dependencies are not accurate, the approach is not viable.

- *Messaging:* draft messaging that can be used to explain the decision being made. Oftentimes, moving a decision from the abstract into core messaging can concentrate minds around the risks and benefits of the approach.

This analysis should be done for each of the two approaches being considered. Typically, the final decision might end up somewhere between the two initial options—certain identified risks mitigated by taking a slightly different approach, for example. This type of structured analysis of potential options achieves a number of important goals. It pushes the boundaries of available options potentially revealing new options, helps the team explore two competing strategic options (which are often advocated for by different team members), and in the end should drive consensus on the best approach and a specific acceptance of whatever risks the best approach requires.

When Is the Crisis Over? Defining Closeout Procedures

Identifying when the team needs to be activated, defining how it will operate efficiently, and working out when the crisis is over are three aspects of effective crisis management. This last aspect of a defined team process may seem the least important, as presumably the worst is over and behind the institution. While the situation is—compared to the other aspects discussed earlier—relatively low stress, it is important that closeout procedures be defined. Just like a good book, any approach to a crisis needs a beginning, a middle, and an end. Not having an end to a book would be highly frustrating and unsatisfying; not having a defined end to a crisis management process raises more challenging risks.

Certainly, no one wants the crisis management process to be unnecessarily prolonged, and if there are no substantive decisions to be made, it is likely that the ongoing stewardship of the issue can be delegated to a special team or back to the college or defined team to manage going forward. But the decision to deactivate the CMT needs to be a deliberate decision made by the team—just as it carefully decided whether or not activation was required at the start of the crisis. It should not be a de facto decision, forced on the process by the unplanned absence of key team members, who have decided to opt out, viewing their time as better spent elsewhere.

In some cases, it is clear when the crisis is "over" from a response perspective. While there might be ongoing "noise" from stakeholders or the media, there are no more substantive decisions to be made. Things may need to be done—and the team may need to get some kind of briefing on developments so that they remain in the loop—but the issue or event is no longer one that requires focused attention and prioritization above other institutional objectives.

In other cases, however, it is not clear that the crisis is over, and yet the process starts to atrophy. This happens when some key team members decide that their time is better spent elsewhere and just voluntarily opt out of the process, perhaps sending a delegate who does not have decision-making authority. It will not be long thereafter when the entire process collapses, leaving one or two people still trying to solve problems, but without the ability or authority to do so. If this occurs when there are still unresolved strategic issues and significant external scrutiny, it can lead to missteps, poor decisions, slow or no response, and it can have a detrimental and lasting impact on the perception of the institution's response. It can inadvertently turn what would have been manageable into another crisis.

Aside from having addressed all the key issues and identified a team or special working group to continue to work the issue, there is one more thing the CMT should do. It should make every attempt to learn from what it has just gone through, with the belief that "those who do not learn from history are doomed to repeat it." "Lessons Learned" procedures are baked into all sorts of operational and incident response plans, yet are often forgotten about or have their importance marginalized when it comes to crisis response and team leadership.

Questions that are good to ask include:

- Did we find out about the issue or event early enough?
- Did we have the right expertise and decision-makers on the team?
- How well did we anticipate risks as the event or issue continued?
- Have we addressed all the questions this issue raised, and have we taken steps to ensure that the issue does not arise again?
- How well did we understand the expectations of our stakeholders?
- Is there anything that we would do differently if we had to do it again?

Implementation Challenges

There are a number of reasons why implementing a defined management process is harder than it should be at most organizations. First, there is often a misplaced confidence that the Crisis Management Team knows what it is doing and how it will operate, no further guidance required. The second is that some of the details of the process can seem rather straightforward. Simplicity in this case is not valued for its own sake but because it can potentially undermine the perceived value of the approach. Thirdly, and perhaps most importantly, crises do not, fortunately, occur that often (an institution may need to employ this type of disciplined approach once a year), and as a result, teams tend to start from scratch every time in terms of the methodology. Crisis management is a perishable skill—a skill that without practice will atrophy.

Chapter 6

Effective Crisis Management IV: Crisis Communications

What Are We Going to Say?

The fourth component of effective crisis management is crisis communications. Given that the two are often confused, this chapter focuses explicitly on crisis communications. Explaining in a consistent and credible way an institution's response is not only critical but will also be the major determinant in shaping how the institution and its leadership will be perceived. Communications is the point at which the proverbial "rubber meets the road"—where the decisions made by the school become public, and stakeholders react either favorably or disapprovingly.

A premium must be placed, therefore, on understanding the perspective, the expectations, and the information needs of the range of stakeholders who are impacted by the institution's decisions. While certainly the communications function has no monopoly on the truth regarding an institution's values and how that needs to be incorporated into the strategy, communicators are probably those most attuned and capable of answering the question, "How will this play out?" or "How will this be perceived?"

Poor crisis response is almost guaranteed when Communications is not at the table when decisions are being made, leaving them in the unenviable position of having to "explain" potentially poor decisions, which will not withstand stakeholder scrutiny. Likewise, a botched communications strategy—whether due to poor messaging, poor spokespeople, bad timing, or inaccurate and confusing information—can undermine even the best-laid plans.

Crisis Communications Is More than Media Relations

Oftentimes, crisis communications is reduced to media relations: How are we going to answer questions from the press, whether from the school newspaper or an agenda-setting national outlet? This reaction is understandable for a number of reasons:

- By the point that reporters are asking questions, we have to recognize that the institution is going to face increasing external scrutiny.
- Media have significant influence in shaping stakeholders' perception of an institution, particularly those less closely associated with it.
- Poor answers to tough questions can quickly lead to a perception of a poor or inadequate response.

These reasons notwithstanding, it is important to distinguish between the potential impact media can have and formulating an optimal communications strategy. Focusing a communications strategy on media relations is inherently a tail-wagging-the-dog strategy, which typically leads to a response that doesn't answer the needs of critical stakeholders and will often lead to the criticism that the administration is more concerned about the media than the underlying issue or event of concern. Faculty will often complain, for example, that they learn more about

Communications at the Table

Marketing and communications professionals, ironically, are often unable to explain the value and strategic insight they bring to an organization's core decision-making. This fact, coupled with the belief that communications lacks the discipline of the law, the analytical precision of finance, or the "finger on the pulse" of Student Affairs, means that administration leaders tend to undervalue or even discount the team's advice in responding to issues or crises. That would be a mistake.

Communications' operational function is to communicate information about decisions that have been made. Communications' strategic function is to provide insight into the reputational risk associated with specific decisions and the likely response by both internal and external stakeholders, in order to inform and influence the decisions being made.

Over the last decade or so, the core competencies of the marketing and communications function at many institutions has leaned away from the old "newsroom" model to preference for investment in resources and talent to execute sophisticated branding campaigns. The change, driven primarily by the imperative to survive in a competitive market and to differentiate the (typically) student experiences from one another, has led in many instances to situations in which the vice president of MarComm or the Chief Marketing Officer may have little or no issues and crisis experience.

This potential gap needs to be recognized and filled, either by elevating the equivalent of the university spokesperson onto the CMT or bringing in outside expertise and support. Regardless of official title or role, if an institution is going to withstand the withering scrutiny of an industry seemingly under fire from all directions, communications must have a seat at the decision-making table.

the administration's response from the local or school newspaper than they do from the institution's leadership, a challenge that is exacerbated in a crisis.

The motivation, alleged by an institution's critics, for focusing more on media than other stakeholders, is that the administration is primarily concerned with "protecting its reputation." Ironically, such a media-centric approach not only damages reputation but also tends to undermine trust in leadership. The flip side of the same coin also explains the challenge raised in the first chapter—that protecting reputation is viewed as unsavory or inappropriate because it is often conflated with having to deal with the media.

Rather than focusing on media relations, the institution's communications strategy should take a "stakeholder-centric" approach, which requires answering the following questions:

- Which stakeholders are most impacted by the issue or event?
- What do they need to hear about the event/issue and the administration's response?
- Who is the most credible and trusted spokesperson on that issue?

A "stakeholder-centric" approach tends to

- identify the issues and information needs of stakeholders, whom the institution really need support from over time;
- allow stakeholders to hear directly from leadership first, without the typically more negative intermediary of media serving as the conduit of information;
- reduce the criticism that the approach is driven by external criticism of reputation rather than concerns about the stakeholders themselves; and
- more likely than not, satisfy stakeholders concerned about the administration's "transparency."

Effectively focusing on the information needs and concerns of key stakeholders also tends to reduce media interest in an issue, which is generally far more interesting if there is either a perception that the administration is hiding some information or that significant factions of the community are opposed to the approach, or if the issue runs counter to the values of the institution. If none of the above is true, reporters will most likely not view the issue as something worth covering. For the press, good news is not news.

Case Study: A Stakeholder-Centric Approach

Two different institutions face the same challenge but take remarkably different approaches with very different results. They discover that an employee has been credibly accused of abusing children who attend the university's daycare facilities.

School 1 faced with this information does the following:

- Fires the employee, informs staff, and initiates new training
- Within twenty-four hours has identified all parents, past and present, who had children in the care of the employee
- Hired a firm that specializes in child abuse prevention to review its policies, physical set up, training, etc.
- Wrote a letter to all parents about what happened and what the school planned to do
- Held a series of meetings with concerned parents, made sure they were aware of resources available to them
- *Outcome.* Media learned about the event and wrote one short, positive piece about the school's response.

School 2, faced with essentially the same information, takes a different approach:

- Fires the employee but does not provide any information to the community, leading to various rumors

- Does not attempt to identify or notify any parents
- Does not conduct any external review or notify law enforcement or child protective services
- *Outcome.*
  - Parents and staff learn of the case three months later, from TV reports that the child abuser has been arrested, and this facility is mentioned as one of the places he had worked for five years.
  - Media coverage is ongoing and highly critical and is focused on lack of administration response.
  - Head of childcare resigns, graduate student and faculty relations are damaged, and civil litigation follows.
  - School closes down childcare center completely and offers access to third-party option as a "risk management" response.

Taking a stakeholder-centric approach to decision-making as taken by the first school—putting the concerns and information needs of parents first—is a simple example of reducing reputational risk to the institution and, at the same time, creating a positive perception of the institution's response to the event or issue. The converse is true also.

The sheer number of stakeholder groups—students, faculty, staff, parents, alumni, corporate partners, legislators, local community groups, the board, not to mention the media—coupled with the pressure and time constraints of social media, highlights the importance of having key aspects of effective crisis communications defined well in advance. This is particularly important because day-to-day responsibility for communicating with these various stakeholders frequently resides in parts of the university that may not routinely coordinate or work together effectively.

The Difference between Emergency Communications and Crisis Communications

Just as crisis communications is far broader than media relations, so too is strategic communications more encompassing than operational communications, which can and should be handled at the emergency response level in the organization. The difference is as important as the distinction between crisis management and emergency management, discussed earlier. Too often this distinction is blurred or not appreciated.

Emergency communications are important to campus safety through the sharing of timely, factual information—this part of campus is closed; there is police activity in the area, stay clear; this building is in lockdown, and so on. This type of communication—often shared via mass alert systems to faculty, students, staff, and sometimes parents who have specifically opted in—in addition to providing basic information is required to conform with Clery Act notifications. It should be owned and managed by Public Safety or the university Police Department and is, essentially, operational.

Crisis communications, on the other hand, despite having a name that seems to mean the same as emergency communications, is completely different and more complex. Rather than conveying information and instruction, it demonstrates values; rather than saying what happened, it explains how the institution is going to respond. Critically, crisis communications is required for all issues or events, and specifically reputational or "self-inflicted" crises, when there is no physical or emergency communication required.

The Importance of Consistent Messaging in a Multi-Stakeholder Model

A university's marketing and communications function is often the hub of communications in what can be an extended hub-and-

Failure in Emergency Communications
Can Become a Crisis

Emergency notification in the case of an active shooter is foundational. If you can't communicate that information in a timely manner, lives could be lost, reputational damage will be significant, lawsuits will proliferate, and heads will rightly roll. Student safety is paramount and a baseline assumption.

Unfortunately, many schools still have problems with emergency notification, either failing to notify in a timely manner or issuing alerts and alarming the entire community when in fact nothing is happening on campus. While no failure has been quite as dramatic as the State of Hawaii's Emergency notification that a North Korean missile was heading toward the islands when it was not, mistakes are frequently made.

One institution, in close proximity to an actual mass shooting event, erroneously alerted the community not once, but three times, that the same shooter was on the campus, when he had in fact already been killed. Parents were irate, students were upset, protocols were reviewed, and personnel changes were made.

At another institution, a student (in a poorly considered prank even for a nineteen-year-old), just days after another mass shooting, ran up and down the halls of the dorm saying there was an active shooter. One student, on hearing this, called his parents, who in turn called local police, who descended en masse on the unsuspecting campus. General mayhem ensued, and at no point was anyone informed of the status. Parents were irate, students were upset, protocols were reviewed, and personnel changes were made.

Every institution should ensure that

- its emergency notification system is tested frequently;
- preapproved messaging is in place for a range of emergencies;
- the authority and ability to make an emergency notification is clear; and
- escalation processes to campus leadership are defined and understood.

spoke model, parallel in many ways to the highly fragmented composition of many colleges and universities. Communications are often managed at multiple levels and in multiple places within the university, including:

- Specific colleges—a challenge particularly in graduate, professional colleges, which often view themselves as distinct from the general undergraduate body
- The Alumni Affairs/Development Office, which often has a significant budget for communications and is focused primarily on one stakeholder group
- The Athletic Department, which is frequently siloed and sometimes viewed as "untouchable"
- Government Affairs, which normally reports into Legal and is a vital channel for public universities
- The Public Information officer, for the university's Public Safety and Police Departments

This complexity is compounded with other vehicles, such as multiple websites (often with different ownership and systems) and multiple social media properties (many of which are not managed by the central communications function). Other functions often interact with important stakeholders, with little direct accountability to the central communications team, including Student Affairs, with various student groups; Human Resources, with employees; and so forth.

These examples are meant to emphasize the point that ensuring consistency in messaging is far easier said than done. And while, in day-to-day operations, discrepancies may be ignored or viewed as not important, during a crisis or significant issue, inconsistencies will be revealed, whether about underlying facts or inferred values. If a media statement says one thing but an officer in the Admissions Department or Alumni Office says something different, the latter will be viewed as representing the "true" perspective of the institution. Contradictions and errors will be portrayed as indicative of an institution that does not know what it is doing, regardless of whether the sources of different information are actually involved in or familiar with the issue in the first place.

The smaller the institution or the more centralized the marketing and communications function, the less problematic this issue will usually be. But a crisis can act like a centrifugal force and will tend to increase pressure and expose gaps in approach, requiring a concerted effort to stop the institution from spinning out of control.

In order to increase consistency in external messaging and create the impression of "one institution" responding in a clear and concerted manner, it is important to establish a cross-functional Crisis Communications Team that is separate and distinct from the university's Crisis Management Team. If the CMT tries to handle all of these communications or worries about wordsmithing activities, it will be failing to do its job. A crisis communications plan, the critical fourth component of effective crisis management, needs to achieve certain specific objectives.

Establish a Cross-Stakeholder Crisis Communications Team. Just as consistency and predictability in approach is necessary at the crisis management level, so too is it vital in crisis communications. The Crisis Communications Team must be broader, by definition, than the communications functions, for which the marketing/communications team is responsible. Key communicators in impacted operational areas of the university must be at the table to

- inform the communications strategy based on the information needs of their stakeholders;
- be aware of the overall strategy and rationale behind any decisions;
- introduce ostensibly unrelated issues that could impact the credibility of the response; and
- reduce duplication of effort and help ensure a consistent approach.

Clearly Define Authority to Approve Messaging. The overall communications strategy and key messaging approach has to be led by the head of central communications, even if in normal times the chief communicator for the college or hospital or other part of the institution would be responsible for getting messaging approved. In a crisis, this person must have the authority to distribute all messaging, even if it is ostensibly coming from a different department. The CMT needs to have overall authority for the communications strategy and high-level messaging, but that is not the same as needing to approve every derivative document that effective communications may require.

Establish the Importance of a Calendar of Events. Crises do not occur in a vacuum, and it is vital to know what else is happening on campus. Unrelated events or announcements can have a profound impact on the perceived priorities of the administration during a crisis. Unless specifically approved, during a crisis all communications—even those ostensibly unrelated to the primary issue—should be put on hold until specifically evaluated for appropriateness given the context. This is an ongoing process and is a natural continuation of the screening process described in chapter 3.

Ensure a Process for Developing and Distributing Shared Messaging and Hard Q&As. It is impossible to be consistent in messaging if frontline staff are not given the talking points and answers to questions they need to consistently respond to inquiries. The communications that will typically need to be developed in a crisis are

- high-level talking points for all administration leaders;
- FAQ, or Frequency Asked Questions, which can be shared broadly, including on a website;
- hard Q&As, which are not broadly distributed but are used for a number of important purposes.

These "hard Q&As" and the administration's possible inability to develop an effective and persuasive response to them can reveal unresolved strategic questions that over time will need to be addressed. The process of developing hard Q&As can, therefore, serve a valuable role in driving a proactive approach and strategy. They can be used for media and meeting preparation and will be particularly useful if contentious meetings with key internal stakeholder groups is anticipated; leadership will need to be prepared to provide answers in response to complex and challenging questions.

Create a Clear Channel for Answers to Unanticipated Questions/ Developments to Be Escalated. Problems arise when well-meaning staff members attempt to answer questions from their stakeholders for which they are not prepared or simply do not have the information. It needs to be clear to whom unexpected questions need to be referred to formulate an appropriate response. In many cases, these questions will have been anticipated (see hard Q&A above) but the answers not proactively shared because they might be inherently problematic.

Ensure that Media and Social Media Guidelines are in Place. The rules of the road need to be clear for everyone:

- How should faculty and staff respond if they get media inquiries?
- What is appropriate to post on social media about the issue?
- Who is officially speaking on behalf of the institution?

Handling Incoming Communications

Frequently so much effort is placed on defining what the institution wants to say, who is going to say it, and the best channels to use (website, campus email, media statement, town hall, video, etc.) that it is easy to forget that effective communications is about listening and responding to stakeholders effectively, too. The biggest challenge many institutions have is that they are not set up to respond to incoming inquiries from stakeholders—be they concerned parents, alumni, or students.

Incoming communications can come from many directions—essentially anywhere there is a publicly listed telephone number or email, which at some institutions, due to publicly listed directories, is literally everyone. Certainly, the main switchboard, the President's Office, Media Relations, the Alumni Office, and Admissions are frequent channels that can quickly become overwhelmed during a crisis.

Phone systems cannot handle the volume, frontline staff don't actually have the answers, and particularly if the crisis is caused by a social or political issue that catches the attention of the media, people completely unaffiliated with an institution (albeit claiming to be about to "enroll my child" or "make a significant donation"!) can and do overwhelm an institution's ability to respond to stakeholders it really cares about.

Other pressure points are often the school's main website, which can go down, simply unable to handle the unexpected peak in traffic, far beyond normal volumes; email systems can get completely jammed up, particularly email alias's like president@. All these challenges can undermine the perception of the effectiveness of the administration's response, which, as has been discussed earlier, is the determinant of reputational damage. Since effective response is in the institution's control, there are a number of things in this area that are worth understanding before a crisis occurs:

- Do you have a phone system in which a dedicated telephone number can be established to handle multiple incoming calls at the same time?
- Have you identified people across the institution who can staff an ad hoc call center, ideally from disciplines who are used to effectively handling difficult individuals (Student Affairs, Billing, Admissions)?
- Do you have a way to easily distinguish between legitimate stakeholders and politically driven nonaffiliates?

Don't Leave Your Stakeholders in the Dark

Well-prepared organizations often have "dark sites" at the ready for crisis events. These microsites are fully functional, prepopulated pages that can be published almost immediately should the need arise. Hidden on a development server or other publicly inaccessible location, they can be launched with little to no preparation to share accurate and timely information. These sites provide an excellent way to quickly communicate across all your stakeholder groups on particularly thorny issues or in an emergency situation. An issue- or crisis-specific microsite establishes your institution as the primary and authoritative source for information, which has a number of benefits, including:

Getting your story out. When there isn't a clear resource for comprehensive information, gaps are filled with rumors and misinformation. By creating a central hub, your site becomes the "go to" place for key information and updates, taking the wind out of the sails of other, possibly hostile, sources.

Demonstrating that you are in control. One of the most important things that you will be communicating with a microsite is that you are not simply "reacting" to a bad situation but that you are taking responsibility to "make things right."

Signaling transparency. While the information that you are sharing may not always reflect positively on you, by providing the facts—the good, the bad, and the ugly—you demonstrate that you are taking the issue seriously, and you build trust through openness.

Speaking in a different "voice." A microsite indicates that this is not business as usual, and so you can adopt a less formal tone to better communicate your concern, empathy, etc., as appropriate.

Providing frontline staff support. A microsite ensures that you are not completely dependent on frontline staff or supporters, who may have varying levels of expertise and background to tell your story. Instead, your representatives have a few key talking points and a website to which they can refer others for more information.

- Can you quickly establish or launch an existing "dark site" to direct those who want more information about what happened and the institution's response?
- Do you have a way to track calls, emails, and letters across stakeholders so that this data can be used as an important metric to gauge the effectiveness of the institution's response and to understand if things are getting worse or getting better?

When Not Saying Anything Is the Best Strategy

All the recommendations given so far are predicated on the assumption that either the institution has no choice but to communicate about the issue or that it has decided that doing so is in its best strategic interest. It is important to remember, however, that not communicating is also a completely viable and, in some instances, the preferable communications strategy. Not communicating is typically preferable when

- the institutional response raises the profile of an issue unnecessarily or implicitly conveys an importance that it does not warrant; this is particularly true if the president (for whatever reason) feels compelled to publicly discuss an issue that is not on anyone's radar;
- the institution has nothing to say on the issue, and responding in some vague fashion will only lengthen the media cycle or increase the interest of other stakeholders;
- the institution needs to buy time to articulate an appropriate response and is not ready to engage; or
- the institution either has already addressed the issue at some earlier time, and all enquiries (from whatever stakeholder) are best addressed by referring them to previous statements.

Agreeing not to say something is quite different, however, from not knowing what statement the institution would be prepared to share, should changing circumstances require a different approach.

There are other times, however, when the decision to communicate or not is explicitly tied to the broader response strategy and the institution's assessment of risk. An interesting way of considering the options to communicate or not was encapsulated in Ian Mitroff's book *Managing Crises before They Happen*,* in which he modified a framework called the Johari Window, which creates a two-by-two matrix regarding what you know and what others know. This has subsequently been modified again, as shown in the illustration.

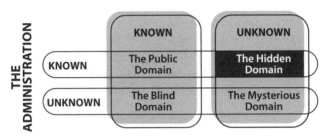

The Case for Saying Nothing

In all areas except for the hidden domain, the administration essentially has no choice about whether to communicate:

- In the "public domain," information is already available, and the administration needs to respond or has already provided information.
- In the "mysterious domain" (a concept best encapsulated by former Secretary of Defense Donald Rumsfeld's description of the "unknown unknowns"), there is nothing to communicate.

*Ian I. Mitroff, with Gus Anagnos, *Managing Crises before They Happen: What Every Executive and Manager Needs to Know about Crisis Management* (Amacon, 2005).

- In the "blind domain," the administration also knows nothing and is thus unable to communicate. Social media has virtually eliminated this domain, as the administration is unable to claim it is unaware.

In the hidden domain, however, the administration is aware of something, but its stakeholders are not, and so it must decide whether or not to communicate about the issue, thereby moving it from being "hidden" to being "public." This is also frequently the space in which reputational risk is most frequently played out and where different perspectives of risk inform decision-making in a crisis.

Not Communicate. Typically, the reason to not communicate in the hidden domain is that no one is currently aware. Thus, by not communicating, no one will find out, and so, best case, the risk essentially disappears; by the point at which it does become public, it may be viewed as old news and irrelevant. Additionally, there is considerable risk to communicating proactively because disclosure itself will create reputational damage for the institution, and the institution will have to do whatever is necessary to solve the problem and repair the damage, once acknowledged.

Another situation in which the optimal strategy may be to not communicate results from the complications created by ongoing and sometimes multiple levels of investigations—whether internal (e.g., Title IX) or potentially criminal. In such cases, communicating publicly could undermine the progress of these various investigations, which in turn could create its own set of reputational damage. This approach, however, is primarily a question of timing—at some point, the institution will need to explain what has occurred. The appropriate response regarding ongoing investigations is actually easier in the hidden domain than when it is in the public domain, when failure to acknowledge even the existence of an investigation—particularly when it is known to be under way—without disclosing any specifics at all can inadvertently create the impression that the institution is trying to hide something or is not taking the allegations seriously.

Communicate. While no one is currently aware now, a realistic assessment suggests that the situation will change and information will inevitably leak. Moreover, it is believed that the legal liability and reputational damage will only be increased by hiding this information, particularly if it is combined with failing to remedy the situation. As a result, the better option for the institution is to communicate about the issue proactively, on its own terms, and to demonstrate accountability and a determination to fix the problem.

Being in the hidden domain does provide the institution the luxury of time—essentially, time to resolve the issue in such a manner that it does not become a crisis. By using the time to develop a comprehensive and credible approach to the underlying issue, at the point of disclosure the institution has—and it appears that it has—taken the situation seriously, has addressed the underlying problems, and is communicating at an appropriate time. This course of action is, of course, not without risks—crisis management is often about choosing the least bad option. Aside from the specifics of the issue or incident, disclosure of something in the hidden domain can raise unrelated uncomfortable questions: "What else are you not telling us?"

The decision about what, when, and if to communicate about a particularly problematic issue is a key strategic decision of the crisis management team. Very rarely will the "not communicate" strategy be successful in today's media and social media environment, and the lack of communication will create the impression of an institution that is trying to hide the truth and unwilling to address the underlying problem. That is a position from which it is almost impossible to recover.

FOIA

While social media has reduced the "hidden domain" to almost zero, another consideration, particularly for public institutions, is the Freedom of Information Act (FOIA) and state-specific equivalents. An interested party—a reporter, a political activist group—can ask for pretty much any type of internal communication and document, whether or not they were intended for public consumption—moving potentially uncomfortable communications into the public domain.

A good example of this difficulty was presented when emails between the head of Media Relations and the head of Marketing at a large public university were FOIAed (now a verb, due its prevalence!), revealing discussions that were critical of conservative lawmakers in the state. In the climate of conservative criticism of left-wing bias on campus, outrage ensued, and both staff members had to resign.

Due to the potential for this type of fallout, in a more publicized story, the chancellor of another large public university resigned, ostensibly after having deliberately used her private email and encouraged her team to use private email in order to skirt risks associated with FOIA. Soon thereafter, the FOIAed emails were released, revealing a host of disagreements between the chancellor and the board on a range of personnel and strategic issues.

Challenges Created by Social Media

In the first chapter of this book, I described social media as a game changer, a suite of technologies that allows information to be easily and almost instantaneously found, shared, and connected in a manner that should put reputation and reputational risk on the front burner of strategic considerations. Social media has shortened the time viewed by stakeholders (and particularly students) as appropriate to respond—what was a day in the newspaper age, turned to hours with the advent of CNN and

Pros and Cons of Commissioning a Special Investigation

One of the most common strategies when in the "hidden domain" is to announce an investigation as part of the institution's demonstration that it will get to the bottom of what happened. It has the advantage of appearing decisive; it reveals the underlying problem with a commitment to fix it; and it has the benefit of providing a reasonable justification for not having the answers to various questions and for not yet having taken specific steps that stakeholders may ask about.

The downside of this strategy, however, is that all the institution has really done is punt the issue to some future point in time. The hard decisions remain and will at some point need to be made; more information may reveal previously unknown but broader or systemic issues in addition to the cause of the investigation. Time will increase expectations for decisive action, and scrutiny from all stakeholders, including the media, will increase as they await the outcome of the investigation. At the end of this process, the institution is likely to be facing the same strategic choice as it was at the beginning—aware of information that could be highly problematic to the institution but that is unknown to stakeholders.

cable news, and is now just minutes in the world of Twitter, Facebook, and Instagram.

At the same time that social media has put more pressure on institutions to quickly respond, it has also created valuable tools to allow a communications team to move from the anecdotal to a data-driven assessment of community sentiment, saliency of issues, and attitudes regarding the effectiveness of the administration's response. Social media can, therefore, be an invaluable tool to inform the broader response and approach, to identify new issues (if not already flagged), and to course-correct strategy before it is too late.

On balance, social media has added tremendous variability, and hence risk and uncertainty, to crisis response; it is almost impossible to gauge whether an issue is going to immediately evaporate or blow up.

For most institutions, the increased transparency and awareness created by social media is the heart of the challenge. Ten years ago, if a professor made a racist or inappropriate comment,

---

Breakout: Social Media and Protest Management

The image of a police officer casually pepper-spraying UC Davis students who were sitting down in protest at tuition increases and social inequity was one of the first social-media driven crises; it generated thousands of "Casually Pepper-Spray Everything Cop" memes (a term in 2011 that was not in the popular lexicon in the way it is today and which actually needed to be explained.)* The memes ranged from Botticelli to the Beatles' *Abbey Road* album cover, from Picasso to Leonardo de Vinci's *Last Supper*.

Just the day before at UC Berkeley, at one of a number of Occupy Wall Street protests, a police officer had broken a student's arm with a baton. Aside from some local news coverage, the event was unremarkable. Objectively, the police activity the day before at Berkeley was more severe (pepper spray being one of the lowest "use of force"), but social media—particularly Facebook, Reddit and Twitter, made the UC Davis pepper spray incident an international phenomenon.

The perception of the response to peaceful protests, fueled by social media, caused long-term damage to the credibility of its new chancellor, Linda Katehi. She resigned five years later, in large part due to the continued fall-out of that incident and specifically allegations that the university had paid social media consultants $175,000 to proactively suppress the Google search results of UC Davis Pepper Spray so that it would not continue to impact the reputation of the school. It backfired.

*See https://www.mercurynews.com/2011/11/23/obrien-how-one-students-pepper-spray-photo-became-an-internet-meme/.

---

only those in the room would be aware of it. Today, that same comment might be posted on a personal Facebook page and subsequently become public; or it might be caught on an iPhone and immediately shared. Social media has essentially reduced the "blind domain"—where there is some limited level of public awareness, but the administration is unaware—to zero. Making no response is rarely an option, and the administration can be spun into crisis mode almost instantaneously while trying to understand the facts of the situation and what, if anything, it should do or say in response.

There are two solutions to this common problem. The first is the development of the incident-screening process defined in chapter 4, to ensure that social media–driven risks are promptly escalated and evaluated—depending on context, severity, saliency of issue, and so on—for the appropriate level of institutional response. Leadership teams that convene to address social media issues, or respond to a provocateur, probably do not have a well-calibrated incident-screening and evaluation process.

The second is to ensure that, for social-media driven issues, the communications function has a rapid-response approach in place. That allows appropriate response without derailing executive leadership, which can otherwise spend too much time in firefighting mode. To be effective, a rapid response capability requires

- focus and monitoring on the issues in question;
- understood guidelines on approach, tone, and language, as well as on when engaging is going to be counterproductive and make the issue worse (see guidelines below);
- preapproved range of optional responses to the identified list of issues;
- defined accountability/authority to respond as staff deem fit within defined parameters;
- comfort level with capabilities, common sense, and experience of staff in the rapid response function; and

- defined escalation points, that is, when the incident has exceeded the authority level of rapid response and may need either additional input from the head of communications or potentially go back to the screening group for further evaluation of the need to convene a meeting of the broader CMT.

Breakout: The Risk of Overreacting to Social Media

A photo of an incoming student is shared on Instagram showing the student smiling, wearing black face and the n-word imposed over the image. Criticism ensures on social media and various groups demand that the administration rescind the offer of the student as the image is offensive and against community values. The school is a public university and so believes the image, while offensive is protected by the first amendment and so that they have no recourse. When the administration is finally able to reach out to the student in question, they learn that the image has been doctored—it was a photo of the 18 year old with a charcoal face mask that was posted years prior and the n-word was superimposed later by someone unknown to the student.

For any institution, social media must be an integral part of the crisis communications approach and include:

Monitoring, including issue-specific search terms to capture posts and discussion that the social media team would not normally be concerned about. To the extent that social media reports help the communications team and more broadly the CMT with strategy, decide how frequently these reports should be shared.

Removing of posts on university-managed properties that violate existing social media policies. Typically, this should allow for the removal of posts that are deliberately inflammatory, untrue, or irrelevant to the primary thread. It is important that decisions to delete any post be made in consultation with the Legal Department and be based on a review of the institution's existing social media guidelines.

Responding, as with the broader discussion above, about when it can be counterproductive to publicly respond to an issue; this question may be relevant at a more tactical level twenty times a day among the social media team. The US Airforce developed one of the first social media response protocols,* which has subsequently been tailored and tweaked by many organizations. Essentially, it provides a clear rationale for when it is either advantageous or counterproductive to respond, based on the type of post, which it divides into the following:

- *Trolls:* which are negative/hateful and for which monitoring (or removal) is the only answer
- *Ragers:* just ranting and for which monitoring is the answer
- *The Misguided:* in which facts or understanding is wrong, and there is an opportunity to correct misinformation by directly responding
- *Unhappy Customers:* someone who has a legitimate bad experience, is sharing it, and can be mollified by engagement and potential action

Clearly, those responsible for social media must have common sense and good judgment and be empowered to respond in a way that diffuses tensions or clears up misunderstanding. The social media representative is a key member of the broader crisis communications team and must be familiar with the overall communications strategy and objectives.

Even with a clear process in place, the challenges of responding to social media are asymmetric: critics can post something

*See https://www.wired.com/2009/01/usaf-blog-respo/.

and demand an instantaneous response, but the institution has a responsibility to assess the accuracy of the information before responding—often leading to a criticism that the administration is too slow or doesn't care.

Given the complexity of effectively responding to issues or crises, it is easy to view communications as the only component that matters—and certainly in the middle of a crisis it is easy for communications requirements to overwhelm the leadership team and potentially prevent them from being successfully oriented to their forward-looking strategic role. To be successful, all components of crisis management must be in place.

While the fourth component of effective crisis management, communications, certainly is the "tip of the spear"—a critical, visible, and impactful part of crisis management—it should not be mistaken for the whole. From a crisis management standpoint, processes must also be in place to support timely reporting and assessment of issues and events; there must be clearly defined roles and responsibilities for different teams based on type of response necessary; and clear tools and processes to support effective decision-making at times of high stress must be in place. Without these capabilities in place, you have—to continue the analogy—the equivalent of the tip without the spear, which will have no momentum, direction, or impact. Your institution's response will not only be slow, unresponsive, unclear, and inconsistent, but the reputational damage will be unnecessarily severe and beyond the capability of any communications team to explain away.

Chapter 7

Redefining Issues Management

You can't build your reputation on what you are going to do.

—Henry Ford

The majority of this book has focused on aligning best practice regarding crisis management; how to align the operational, strategic, and communications aspects of response; ensure a strategic and proactive approach to get ahead of a crisis; prevent common challenges from occurring through the definition of a defined management process that mitigates those risks; and clearly establishing the role of communications and the importance of taking a stakeholder-centric approach to decision-making.

The methodology and concepts essential to effective crisis management are also fundamental to effective issues management, which ideally takes place earlier along the issues-to-crisis continuum described in chapter 1. The real promise of issues management—the time- resource-and-reputation-saving strategy—is proactive identification and mitigation of issues. It's the early warning system that allows an institution to course-correct before an issue becomes a crisis. As such, it is critical that universities transition their issues management approach from after-the-fact communications response to proactive identification, prioritization, and management.

Unfortunately, that is not the case at most institutions. In fact, most issues that schools prioritize are part of the recovery strategy related to a crisis the school has recently experienced. For example, initiatives to strengthen Title IX programs are typically part of an institution's recovery strategy following high-profile sexual assault cases. Investments in enhanced cyber security IT infrastructure are made after personal information has been compromised, and campus climate initiatives around diversity after egregious racial incidents. Unfortunately, this type of issues management, while important, is by definition reactive. It's a "barn door–closing initiative" after all the horses have bolted—a prudent step, but essentially too late.

The Luxury of Time: A Blessing and a Curse

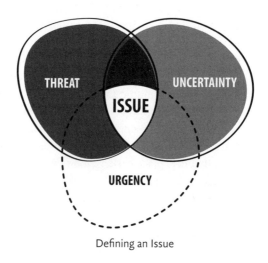

Defining an Issue

In chapter 1, a crisis was defined as the intersection of a threat, uncertainty, and urgency. An issue, on the other hand, has two of those components—threat (an issue that, if left unaddressed, could pose significant reputational damage to your institution) and uncertainty (the solution is not clear and may impact other priorities), but what is missing is the sense of urgency.

Time can be a blessing and a curse. It allows the institution to make more measured decisions; to evaluate the risks and uncertainties in a more deliberate and analytical way, to develop a more coherent and consistent communications strategy, and to explain to stakeholders the steps the institution is taking and

Don't Be Lulled into Inaction by Slow-Moving Issues

Consider the fable of the frog in boiling water. If you drop a frog in a pot of boiling water, it will of course frantically try to clamber out. But if you place it gently in a pot of tepid water and turn the heat on low, it will float there quite placidly. As the water gradually heats up, the frog will sink into a tranquil stupor, exactly like one of us in a hot bath, and before long, with a smile on its face, it will—without resisting—allow itself to be boiled to death.

why. But all too frequently, because of the lack of urgency, an issue gets put on the back burner. Unlike a crisis, there is no defined, cross-functional team assigned to mitigate the risk, and there are no goals or milestones to meet. Ultimately, nothing gets done. It is of course possible that the issue just goes away. More likely, however, the issue continues to fester, ignored or already rationalized internally, until it's too late.

Now a crisis, the previously manageable issue leaves the administration looking reactive and insensitive to the underlying event. Leadership credibility is compromised, the issue is compounded, and the needed response is likely going to be significantly greater—more costly in time, resources, and reputation—than if the issue had been proactively addressed. And like a crisis, the perceived (in)effectiveness of the response can have more influence on reputation than the issue itself.

Industry in the Cross Hairs and Understanding Prevailing Narratives

Some of the dynamics that are roiling campus communities—mishandled sexual assault investigations, acts of "free"/hate speech either ignored or blown out of proportion, the increasing perception of inequity between lucrative administrative positions and poorly paid and underappreciated adjunct faculty and debt-laden students—are not specific to any one campus. Rather, they are "industry" issues—and in many cases societal issues, which are as relevant on as off-campus—that threaten the reputation of higher education itself.

While an individual institution may not currently face any of these specific challenges, it is important to understand that these themes are part of a broader and prevailing narrative about higher education. The concept of "prevailing narrative" is important for understanding issues management specifically but communications more broadly. Essentially, absent some significant and abrupt change in event, the prevailing narrative will be confirmed by related, new information. For example, the prevailing narrative about Title IX is that sexual assault is common in higher education and that schools do too little to combat it.

In 2014, a *Rolling Stone* article, "A Rape on Campus," about a gang rape by a fraternity at University of Virginia, was given a credence it did not merit because it aligned with the prevailing narrative—that of course events like this happen on college campuses all the time. It was subsequently retracted in full and caused significant damage to the reputation of that publication.

It is extremely difficult to create a compelling and believable counter-narrative once one narrative has been established. That's why it is important in issues management to understand the potential impact of these broader industry "trends." If one of these issues hits the headlines, will an institution be given the benefit of the doubt? Absolutely not.

Not being given the benefit of the doubt does not mean, however, that all is lost. Although it is an uphill climb, demonstrating that the institution acted promptly, was true to its values, made hard decisions, and tried to provide stakeholders with accurate, consistent information about the incident and its response can protect institutional reputation.

One concrete way leadership teams can start to grapple with these societal and industry issues is to regularly carve out time during board or leadership team meetings to review recent events: What if [enter topic issue X] had happened here? Are we prepared? Are our policies clear? Is there anything the institution should do now to mitigate this risk and prepare for anticipated stakeholder scrutiny?

Step 1: Issue Identification

In an ideal world, a school will commission research specifically focused on identifying, understanding, and prioritizing the issues that matter to your key stakeholders—students, alumni, faculty, parents, trustees, and staff—as well as broader questions around trust and credibility.

- What do stakeholders actually know about the institution?
- Do stakeholders trust the institution and its leadership?
- How would stakeholders describe your school's values? And are you meeting them?
- Are there specific issues about which stakeholders are most concerned?
- What would make stakeholders change their opinion of your institution on specific issues?

It is rare, however, for a school to do this type of reputational research with scarce resources dedicated to supporting brand and marketing efforts—to "building" as opposed to "protecting," to inform marketing strategies and campaigns regarding student enrollment, competitive differentiation, and, to a lesser extent, fundraising/capital campaigns. This important type of research is certainly required before spending significant sums on brand and marketing campaigns. With defined return-on-investment metrics, there is clearly a business case to be made for the value of this type of research.

The general lack of metrics and "return" on broader reputation or issues management research perhaps explains why it is rarely conducted. Instead, consider information the school may have already gathered, albeit for different purposes. Have staff/faculty employment satisfaction surveys been undertaken? Social and media reports and analysis? Surveys of alumni? Campus climate surveys of students?

The more information available to the team beyond the merely anecdotal, the better. And if the institution has an enterprise risk management program, or is about to start one, what data and analysis from that separate process may be available to help inform the identification of strategic issues? The final list of issues should be tailored to the unique attributes of an individual institution and will depend on a number of variables, including size, private or public, as well as areas of specific risk, such as having a Division 1 athletics program, a research enterprise, or owning and managing affiliated medical centers and networks, etc.

Once an initial list of potential issues has been developed, these issues will need to be prioritized. This process may be informed by empirical research or data that provides a deeper understanding of stakeholder perception, or it may depend on the cross-functional team's internal assessment of the relative strategic importance of each issue. Variables that should be considered in this prioritization include:

- Does the issue potentially impede the institution's ability to execute against its strategic vision?
- Is the issue of concern across all stakeholders or is it only of concern to one particular group?
- Is the issue a trend (expected to grow or diminish over time) or is it an uncertainty?

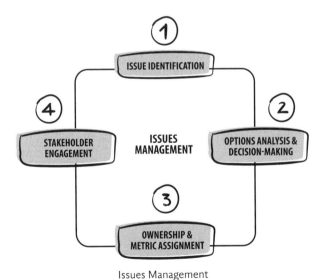

Issues Management

- Is the issue part of a broader narrative currently ongoing in higher education?
- Do any issues present new opportunities?

Who is doing this work? It depends, but for small institutions it could be the Crisis Management Team itself; for larger institutions, an Issues Management Council, or it could be an existing leadership group, if that seems appropriate. The key is for the team to be cross-functional and to make no more than five issues institutional priorities for the coming year; any more than five and it is almost inevitable that little to no progress will be made; any fewer and the focus of the proactive approach will be too narrow.

At the start, it is valuable and sufficient to simply reach consensus among leadership on the top five issues that need to be proactively and strategically addressed without the pressure of a "crisis." As the program matures, however, it is important to remember that the objective of issues management is to look out into the future. What are the issues that, if unaddressed, will start to impact the institution in one or two years, at a minimum. In subsequent cycles of this process, the time frame against which issues are analyzed will get longer, perhaps looking at five years down the line as opposed to those that must be addressed in the upcoming school year.

Step 2: Options Analysis and Decision-Making

With an agreement on the priority issues, the next step is to translate this insight into an assessment of the risk or opportunity each issue presents and to match that to tangible strategic action. Naturally, the inclination will be to focus on the potential reputational vulnerabilities of these issues. However, it is important to recognize that the broader objective is not just to protect against downside risk but to identify opportunities to build on underutilized strengths.

Regardless of the specifics of the issue, the strategic options are normally limited to one of the following four options: Change, Accept, Strengthen, or Educate.

Change

Issues involving change are the hardest to address because they could potentially threaten the reputation of the institution and the credibility of its leadership. Though not currently high profile, the institution believes the issue represents a significant vulnerability if left unaddressed and a proactive approach needs to be taken. The current position is not tenable, cannot be solved through communication, and needs decisive action with clear accountability and established milestones and reporting. It is likely that the majority of the top issues will be those that require a "change" strategy.

Case Study. A school has risen rapidly in the past few years on the list of top party schools. Recently, it has had some close calls and is extremely worried that a death or serious fraternity incident is just around the corner. Moreover, the school's reputation as a leading research institution may be impacted. Based on the risk, it becomes clear that something needs to change before it's too late.

Strategy. The team develops an action and education plan—to put into place new and much stricter oversight of the Greek system and to partner with an organization that educates students on risky behavior. Metrics are established to measure progress over time. While the likelihood of an incident occurring has been diminished, even if it does occur, the reputation of the institution will be inoculated by the proactive steps it has taken.

Accept

On the other end of the spectrum, it is always possible—having looked at the various options and their strategic, financial, and operational impacts—that there are important benefits associated with the risk or that the cost of "solving" the issue is actually higher than the potential cost associated with the risk. The reality is that there are some risks that simply cannot be mitigated and must be accepted. However, it is important to have arrived at this decision consciously and only after careful deliberation.

In accepting this risk, it is imperative that the institution have in place a defined crisis management plan to handle any fallout promptly and effectively if, or more likely when, the crisis results. Specifically, a top issue with an "accept" strategy must be clearly identified and incorporated as a specific criterion into a crisis management's incident-reporting process. Moreover, clear policies should be in place, and reactive messaging (including holding statements, hard Q&As, etc.) on the issue should be developed and approved to expedite response. Though "eyes wide open" is better than comfortable deniability, it is still an inherently risky approach.

Case Study. Through focused hiring of new faculty and pursuing various research grants, the institution has become a research magnet in infectious disease and pandemics. Unfortunately, the groundbreaking work being done on campus involves research on chimpanzees. You've recently received information that PETA and other animal rights organizations are gaining traction on campus. There are no viable research options that do not involve testing on animals.

Strategy. The decision is made that the benefits of this research and the prestige that it brings the school is worth the risk. It ensures strict compliance with and implementation of research protocols for animal research, along with a plan and communication strategy to address the protests that are anticipated within the next six months

Strengthen/Build

Unlike other issues, strengthen/build issues at first appear problematic but present an opportunity. In fact, the school may already be doing something innovative that only comes to light after further research. However, any build strategy must be based on what the institution has already achieved, rather than what it is going to do in the future. The danger of overpromising and underdelivering is a significant risk, which can undermine trust in the institution and its leadership, as well as the believability of other claims. Build strategies, therefore, take time. They can only progress as fast as the institution changes and evolves. The "halo" effect of build strategies, however, can be broad and have positive reputational benefits in unrelated areas.

Case Study. During the final week of a precollege STEM program geared toward middle and high school students, a parent contacts the Office of Student Affairs to express concern about an "overly friendly" instructor. Although the issue, the result of a miscommunication, was quickly resolved, it brings to the fore concerns around child abuse prevention. In a preliminary review, the team realizes that there are a number of programs that put the institution at risk relative to this issue, including an onsite childcare program, summer and holiday programs run by outside vendors, and tutoring and mentoring programs sponsored by the school.

Strategy. While exploring ways to address this issue, the institution realizes that its Title IX program parallels the structures and resources needed for a child abuse prevention program. Moreover, as a result of a painful but constructive Office of Civil Rights review a few years ago, the program is strong, comprehensive, and now well-respected. The team decides to leverage the knowledge and strength of the existing program with extra funds and resources and effectively communicate the steps the school takes to protect against this risk.

Educate

Some issues will be driven by a lack of understanding about the institution, its current approach, and existing policies and programs. Stakeholders may simply be unaware or confused, and clear, effective communications is the primary solution to these issues.

Case Study. Located in an inner-city environment, a school's campus climate is influenced by city events and politics. Recent investigative reports by the local newspaper have exposed rampant racism within the local Police Department, both in hiring and treatment of suspects. The belief is that this is a systemic issue in city government and not restricted to the police. Students on campus have begun organizing and targeting their attention on the administration's admission and hiring policies as a way to "act locally."

While historically this school has not had a stellar record in this area, two years ago they hired a director of Diversity and Inclusion and provided the office with a substantial budget. As a result, a number of policy changes have been implemented, and the school has seen a small but positive uptick in minority enrollment and retention—both in the faculty and in the student body. Your team realizes that these actions, though well known by the administration, have not been widely reported to your stakeholders.

Strategy. The team decides once again to introduce the director to the community along with a presentation of the five-year diversity plan. They also plan a series of campus events to solicit additional student, faculty, and alumni input into future strategy. Increased awareness of what has already been done, the acknowledgment that a great deal more needs to be achieved, and an openness to dialogue and engagement helps reduce tensions on campus.

Financial Modeling in Issues Management: Using the Impaired Asset Model

The impaired asset model, which is typically used to write down the value of an asset on an organization's books that has lost value—can be a useful tool from a strategic decision-making point of view to analyze the potential reputational damage of a specific issue. Certain assumptions, as with any predictive model, have to be made about the nature of the issue, its impact, and its duration. Then, based on these assumptions (declining enrollment, declining philanthropy, etc.), it is possible to calculate reputational risk tied to a specific issue by using a standard discounted cash-flow analysis. Assuming that an event will happen, the financial impact can then be calculated compared to the baseline model if the event or issue did not occur. The difference between the two can then be calculated, which represents the value of the reputational damage caused by the event—assuming it occurred.

This approach has been taken to quantify reputational damage to drive programmatic changes to significantly reduce the likelihood of the event occurring in the first place. A good example is analysis that was conducted by a global financial institution to calculate the impact of a significant data breach on its operations, the outcome of which was sweeping changes in the way the organization assessed and managed that risk. In chapter 5, the importance of developing a planning case was discussed in reference to the delayed construction of the Thirty Meter Telescope on Mauna Kea in Hawaii. Using this kind of financial analysis, the TMT management could have identified a specific dollar value associated with a predetermined delay—a financial calculation that might have impacted the organization's overall strategy.

This approach is useful on particularly large and significant issues, where it is important to support broader strategic questions—with the risk essentially quantified, what are the proactive investments in people, policies, partnerships, support resources, and so on, that are sensible to take in order to reduce the likelihood of that anticipated risk or issue materializing? It can be a highly effective tool, but it needs to overcome three barriers, discussed earlier, regarding a general overoptimism on the part of every organization, that (a) the event won't happen, but (b) if it does, it won't be as bad as we think, and (c) the management team will be able to handle it. The challenge, of course, with high-impact low-likelihood issues or events is that traditional financial analysis tools assign a low probability to the event, which will reduce the net present value of the risk to near zero—suggesting that nothing should be done. Rather, the assumption behind this discounted cash-flow analysis is that the event will happen (even if we don't quite know when). As a result, the analysis supports a broader strategic approach to minimizing reputational damage.

Step 3: Establish Clear Issue Ownership and Metrics

Successful issues management programs require a committed, leadership-level, cross-functional Issues Management Council (IMC) and a clearly defined, rigorous, coordinated, and effective management process. Given the frequent overlap between this group and the CMT, proactive issues management can be identified as a specific responsibility of the CMT. Whatever the exact structure appropriate to each institution, this team should meet on a regular basis—at least quarterly—and be responsible for

- leading the issues identification and prioritization process;
- collaborating on strategies to mitigate top issues;
- establishing clear metrics and issue-specific accountability; and
- assessing progress that issue-specific teams have made against goals.

For an issue to be effectively managed—as opposed to reactively responded to—progress on the project plan must be made even when the issues are not in the spotlight. Clear authority and responsibility, clear reporting, and defined goals and milestones that conform to SMART criteria (Specific, Measurable, Agreed Upon, Realistic, and Time Specific) are necessary.

Incorporating metrics into this process is important for two reasons. First, it provides strategic value by scaling the potential impact of an issue before a triggering event happens. That analysis can then be used to proactively build the case for whatever mitigation steps are required to reduce the likelihood of the event or issue ever occurring in the first place (see Impaired Asset Model discussion, above).

Second, it strengthens management accountability and drives progress on priority issues. Creating a dashboard can help inform decisions about whether program components are actually successful in driving improvement against goals, or it can provide an early warning sign that something is headed in the wrong direction. As the saying goes, What gets measured gets done. For example, metrics for issues around managing diversity and equity issues on campus would include the percentage of minority/underrepresented groups in staff, faculty, and students over time, the number of Title VI investigations, institutional spending with minority firms, campus climate survey data, and so on.

For each of the top five issues, a subteam should be identified, which will also need to agree to the following:

- Who is responsible for leading the issue and has responsibility for driving the project plan?
- What are the defined metrics to measure progress?
- What are the milestones?
- What are the immediate policies, practices, hiring, funding, etc., that need to be favorably resolved to make progress?
- Who are the key stakeholders who should be engaged in this process?
- What modes of engagement (e.g., outreach, team membership) will be required to refine the approach and gain acceptance for implementation?
- What are the immediate and medium-term communications needs for this work to be well positioned and, ultimately, favorably received?

To some, this approach may seem overly complicated and potentially bureaucratic. It certainly does require some time commitment, which is often hard to find owing to the constant pressure of reactively responding to a plethora of issues! But that is the entire point. Rather than constantly reacting, this proactive methodology should, over time, actually reduce the churn and the disruption of always responding to an unexpected issue that is thrown over the transom.

Step 4: Stakeholder Engagement

The role of the communications function in managing an issue or a crisis is essentially the same—a focus on coordinated, consistent, and multi-stakeholder communication to explain the school's position, its programs, and where it is continuing to focus its attention and resources. The only difference, essentially, between an issue and a crisis for the communications team is the degree of speed required and whether the opportunity has been taken to get ahead of the issue by proactively

- developing Issues Briefs that include the institution's point of view, history on the issue and recent developments, as well as holding statements, key talking points, Q&A, and links to other resources (policies, website, etc.);
- developing fact sheets or other materials that clearly demonstrate a track record;
- identifying a media-trained expert on the issue who can persuasively speak with stakeholders, including the media; and
- identifying stakeholders who are supportive of the administration's efforts and willing to speak on its behalf (so called third-party advocates).

Communications, of course, is not just about talking but listening, and stakeholder engagement means a great deal more than speaking at stakeholders. About twenty years ago, this important concept morphed from being referred to as stakeholder "management" to stakeholder "engagement," reflecting recognition that stakeholders, in fact, can't be managed—an improvement in terminology, if not necessarily in the substance of some of the resulting efforts.

The word *engagement* itself has a host of contradictory associations, from the positive, referring to an engagement before marriage, to the negative, denoting a military engagement. The common thread—whether love or war—is the coming together of two distinct forces in which the outcome is uncertain. Genuine stakeholder engagement, likewise, can be similarly risky, which is why it is typically not really pursued in a thorough way; it requires a willingness to engage, to establish a feedback loop, ensuring an active and positive two-way communication with stakeholders, and an openness to change.

In many ways, the issues management program leads to the development of a culture across the institution that can mitigate reputational risk—essentially, to the degree to which the organization's culture, leadership, and strategy is based on a shared understanding of the values and expectations of the stakeholders on whom its ongoing and future success is reliant.

By clearly, effectively, and transparently communicating with each stakeholder group about the administration's thinking and approach to issues that are important and relevant to them, the administration is building a reservoir of goodwill to carry an institution through more challenging times, which are inevitable when dealing with any kind of substantive issue. By increasing mutual understanding, it is highly likely that the institution is effectively *closing the gap between decisions and stakeholder expectations*—the very definition of reputational risk as described in this book.

Chapter 8

The Role of Leadership in Crisis

I'm sitting over a number of dormant volcanoes.
—Wallace Loh, former president of the University
of Maryland, College Park

A New Leadership Playbook for Today's Reputational Crises

When preparing for crises, on many campuses there is an expectation that there will be little to no warning—shots are fired, a tornado touches down. While it is critical to prepare for these events, this focus on what is really emergency management has given colleges and universities a false sense that they have a crisis management capability in place when, in fact, they do not.

As discussed earlier, 90 percent of crises that impact schools—and have the potential to undermine the credibility of the president—are self-inflicted crises. They run the gamut from sexual assault and violence on campus to inappropriate handling of finances and data; from faculty misconduct and academic fraud to intellectual property theft, animal rights, and inappropriate patient care. Unlike terrorism or a natural disaster, in these self-inflicted crises, neither the president nor the institution will be considered a "victim" or viewed as suffering from a terrible event perpetrated by external forces beyond the institution's control.

Self-inflicted crises tend to be the inevitable result of poor decisions or poor oversight, evolving over weeks if not months. As such, they require a completely different approach from crises that are the result of random acts of violence or natural disasters. Relying on a crisis management leadership "playbook" based on an outdated understanding of the risks that face an institution of higher education puts a university and, by default its president, at significant risk.

A president's legacy is determined by how effective he or she was in both building and protecting the reputation of the institution. A poorly managed crisis can end the otherwise storied career of the institution's "CEO," who is the person with overall accountability for what occurs on the campus. Newspapers are littered with examples of presidents who have been either forced out or who, postcrisis, came to the conclusion that they would prefer to "spend more time with their family." But a loss of leadership credibility is not an inevitable outcome of a crisis; rather, it is an inevitable outcome of ineffective crisis management.

In addition to the normal challenges every leader faces, there are three main reasons why the survival rate for university and college presidents in crisis is so low:

1. An academic institution's traditional management model, with its focus on shared governance and consensus building, is uniquely ill-equipped to manage the dynamics of a fast-evolving crisis.
2. Having risen through the ranks of academia, former professors of astrophysics or chairs of the Philosophy Department are suddenly expected to transform into the role of mayor of a small city—a role few are equipped to manage effectively, particularly first-time presidents.

3. Brutal campus politics, unresolved issues, and long-forgotten grievances can become forces unto themselves during a crisis—exacerbating risk, prolonging turmoil, and effectively blocking resolution.

Failure in crisis is not inevitable, however. Indeed, with a little forethought and the right institutional culture, it should be possible for any institution and its leader to survive a crisis with its reputation not only intact but burnished, owing to the quality of the response.

This chapter explores first the key stakeholder relationships that need to be understood and nurtured, specifically, the institution's Board of Trustees and its Faculty Senate; second, proactive steps a president should take to reduce the likelihood of a crisis occurring; and third and finally, the role of the president as the "face" of the institution during a crisis.

The Three-Legged-Stool Analogy of Shared Governance

While tenure, academic freedom, and shared governance are typically the three legs of the stool that support a robust academia, the analogy of the three-legged stool is often also applied, particularly by faculty, to the components of shared governance—the administration, the board, and the faculty. The institution's president—appointed by the board, serving as leader of the administration, and most often also a member of the faculty—has a unique responsibility and challenge to balance these competing centers of influence. This obviously applies to all aspects of running the institution, but the pressures can be uniquely intensified during a time of crisis.

Earlier, we discussed the importance of a stakeholder-centric model for decision-making and communications, but at no time is it more difficult to calculate what that means than when two of the legs of the proverbial stool of shared governance have completely different perspectives on priorities and strategic direction.

The Role of Faculty in a Crisis

Faculty are usually well intentioned and remain at an institution for a long time. Arguably, they and their intellectual contributions embody much of the institutional reputation, and they build relationships with students that can last a lifetime. The fact is, faculty members have a credibility and authenticity that administrators simply will not be given. It is because of their central importance at a university in the first place that faculty can both generate and heighten a crisis.

At its most benign, in a crisis it can be expected that a prominent faculty will in a crisis, regardless of merits, vocally and publicly criticize the administration's response, or a "rogue" professor with a constituency of one will publicly position himself or herself as representing the entire faculty. This kind of sniping, while annoying and occasionally detrimental to the perception of the administration's response, pales in comparison to institutional crises when the administration and the faculty are perceived as working at cross-purposes—most typically, when a school is facing a financial crisis or a strategic realignment.

Faculty everywhere are notoriously resistant to change, and with faculty leaders usually protected by tenure, there are few of the normal levers to enforce change if the faculty is unwilling. Faculty have the power over cooperation—they don't have to cooperate with the board, president, provost, deans, or chairs, and if they aren't effectively influenced to do so, they will not. Most faculty believe that they are the foundation of the university and that they can outlast the president and any initiatives—through non-cooperation, stonewalling, or passing votes of no confidence. This can be made worse if the board and the faculty are at loggerheads. Faculty generally have a longer timeframe—often counter to the short-term urgency the board and administration may feel—and believe that they can delay and outwait any changes they do not support. Just as they do with administrative leadership, faculty believe they will remain long after board members have left, particularly if those members are term limited.

This situation is complicated by the reality that faculty are not monolithic—there are factions within the faculty, and many members simply do not want to get involved in university politics, preferring to focus on their research or academic interests. That dynamic can, unfortunately, result in the Faculty Senate—the ostensible voice of the faculty in shared governance—not truly representing the perspective of faculty more broadly at the institution. The Faculty Senate has an imprimatur of authority and often claims to represent the "true" interests of the institution—while the president and administration team are often portrayed as hapless tools of a corporate board that doesn't understand what a university is all about, and thus should be ignored. While this is a gross overgeneralization, like every cliché, there is an element of truth in it.

This dynamic can create tremendous stress on a president—often a member of the faculty and typically someone who will return to the faculty after serving as president. However difficult or easy it may be to marginalize the faculty's perspective as being out of touch, it is vital, particularly in a crisis, to understand the influence faculty can have on both the perception of the institution and its ability to change. It is, therefore, important for the president to carry out certain actions:

- Pursue a strategy of engagement, by creating opportunities for cooperation and to at least marginalize faculty who may be vocal but unrepresentative critics.
- Show good will, empathy, flexibility, and collegiality, in order to win over the "persuadable majority."
- Recognize early on where your vision for the school represents a shift from long-held institutional values and

recognize that change is hard, and it will likely result both in significant pushback and in slower implementation.
- Ensure that you have a really good provost, who has the trust of the faculty and who supports your vision.

The Japanese concept of *nemawashi* is particularly useful here. Literally, it means digging around the roots of a tree. What it means culturally is spending more time up front socializing ideas, getting feedback, and modifying approaches, so that at the point when a decision is needed, there is less resistance, which speeds up implementation. The tree is successfully transplanted and has the best chance of living in its new location. The ability to achieve this result depends on creating a relationship of trust—and trust, of course, can be more easily lost than won.

The Role of the Board in a Crisis

Boards of universities or colleges have three primary roles:

1. To ensure the financial sustainability and health of the institution
2. To ensure a sound strategic direction
3. To appoint an appropriate and effective leader of the institution

A crisis will often impact all three of these objectives, and frequently the board will either become directly involved in the institutional response to the crisis or may be blamed for the crisis—for failing to choose the right leader, encourage a culture that would have prevented the crisis from occurring, or failing to demonstrate sufficient oversight.

The role of the Board of Trustees at institutions of higher education has never been more important, primarily driven by intense competitive pressures, demographic changes, an unchanging business model, and increasing scrutiny in general of the appropriate stewardship and oversight of the institution.

While there are no doubt exceptions, the fund-raising model of boards, with members who viewed it primarily as a social opportunity, is outdated and insufficient for most schools.

Unfortunately, during a crisis, boards can toggle quickly between being hands-off and rubber stamping the recommendations being made by the administration, to becoming highly concerned and involved at a level of detail in approach and decision-making that moves from its appropriate oversight role to the level of a management role. Neither approach is ideal, and the president is in the unique position of having to navigate changing expectations and demands. Such rapid changes in a board's operating mode generally signal a declining confidence in the leadership team, if not the president specifically. The board will be 100% behind the president until they are not—and that trust, so critical to an effective relationship between a president and the board, can, and does, turn on a dime in a crisis.

Maintaining trust and confidence in the president's leadership style, strategic direction, and crisis acumen by the board is often helped by these measures:

Regularly updating the board chair and/or Executive Committee on emerging areas of reputational risk and potential crises. Some schools, particularly those that have gone through major crises, have their head of communications provide a briefing to the board chair every other week. It gives the board perspective, information, and confidence that the internal team is on top of developments. This helps balance what is typically a finance- or litigation-focused board update process.

Identifying opportunities for shared risk assessment and planning; in some anticipated crises (for example the decisions to close campus due to COVID-19), it can be productive to get a subset of board members involved early on, particularly if a decision will have significant financial impacts; it will speed up response, clarify decision-making, and prevent second-guessing down the line regarding strategy and decision-making.

Clearly defining the coordination process between the administration and the board during a crisis. In cases when the CMT has formally been activated, the CMT leader or president should

- promptly give the board chair the latest information and, as soon as possible, the forecasts of the reputational, legal, operations, and financial impacts;

- confirm that information is shared with the broader board by the chair or via general counsel or secretary to the board; and
- establish a regular briefing cycle, based on the severity of the crisis.

Formalizing this process can help build confidence among board members that the crisis is being appropriately managed and can maintain the CMT's authority to make decisions effectively and expeditiously, except for those specifically singled out as requiring Executive Committee approval.

Consciously scheduling one-on-one meetings with all board members once a year if possible, in addition to normal board schedules. As with any group, it is sometimes the quietest members whom it is most important to hear. This also helps ensure that the president doesn't get a balkanized picture of the board's viewpoint and helps build relationships and goodwill that will be important in times of crisis.

Building effective working relationships with the faculty and with the board can certainly mitigate some of the risks associated with being a president during a time of crisis. Let us now examine three other key areas, aligned with the risks associated with being in a crisis detailed in chapter 2, and the best practice addressed throughout this book.

Priority 1: Before a Crisis: Establish a Culture in Which "Bad News" Is Shared

It is important for every university or college president to establish a culture on campus in which bad news can be shared in a fault-free environment. Too often, however, leaders can become isolated and disconnected from the campuses they lead. While this risk is minimized to some degree on smaller campuses, there can often be cultural barriers that may cause leaders to have an overly optimistic assessment of the state of their institution. This is driven by a number of factors:

The Perils of a Long-Time Presidency

Aside from the first year of a presidency, the second most dangerous time to be president is the last year—and hopefully not the last year due to a crisis. There are significant challenges that presidents need to be aware of as they near the end of a distinguished and successful career:

Board acquiescence. The board is less likely to act as a check on the administration or to scrutinize financial presentations of forecasts related to new initiatives. Things have gone well for so long, why would it suddenly change? After many years of service, presidents are able to effectively manage the board, rather than the other way around. In major crises, often the board chair and key board members are also forced to step down.

Overconfidence in the ability to manage crises. A president who probably has successfully navigated a crisis or two can become overconfident in his or her ability to manage the next one.

Collegiality. While a virtue in cabinet meetings, collegiality can lead to cabinet members being less likely or unwilling to challenge the president's leadership or decision-making style.

Misplaced loyalty. With a leadership team that the president has likely hired, has worked with for decades, and with which he or she has close personal relationships, there is a risk that personal loyalty to the president can override institutional loyalty and objective counsel.

There are benefits of course: a reservoir of goodwill among key stakeholders, built up over years of effective leadership; institutional knowledge that can help put developments in context; and experience about what has worked in the past. No doubt, for every long-time president whose term ended in crisis, there are no doubt examples that show the exact opposite to be true. All things being equal, however, long-tenured leadership increases many of the risks identified in chapter 2 as compounding risk during a crisis.

- Subordinates tend to want to be perceived as competent; therefore, accomplishments and meeting milestones often result in good news overwhelming less optimistic information.
- Bad news, when it is shared, is often portrayed as something that happened in the past but has now been "fixed." Because one individual may not understand the full strategic picture, this dynamic tends to exacerbate the risk of a situation becoming worse and information being received too late.
- The well-known tendency to "shoot the messenger" can lead to chronic underreporting of negative issues.
- The larger the power differential between the person reporting and the person being reported to, the less likely bad news will be shared. This essentially means that the president can often be the last person to find out.

Learning of bad news early on is not only critical to effective crisis management but also paramount to ensuring the trust and confidence the board has in the president. A president can take certain steps to help ensure a culture in which bad news is shared:

- Establish an open-door policy and reputation for taking all concerns seriously—from all stakeholders.
- Do not minimize or disbelieve bad news.
- Trust—but verify—the rosy accounts about the state of the school.

Priority 2: Before a Crisis: Clearly Define the President's Role

If the role of the president is defined as limited to "declaring a disaster" (as it often is in emergency management plans owned by Facilities or Police Departments), and seemingly everything else is going on in the Emergency Operations Center, more definition and thought needs to be given to the role of the president. While this approach clearly understates the important role the president has to play, it is also true that the centrality of the president's role in crisis management is often overemphasized. Indeed, an institution must develop a capability that is separate from the presence of one individual, even the president. This is important for a number of reasons:

Presidents spend increasingly less time on campus. They travel for fundraising and student recruitment, meet with alumni, attend board meetings, legislative meetings, and conferences, or are simply stuck, sitting on the tarmac at an airport to pretty much anywhere! In one instance, a president was fly-fishing in Alaska with major donors and was completely off the grid for three days during a crisis. The need to respond to a crisis cannot be hampered by the unavailability of any one individual, let alone the chief executive.

Presidents can exacerbate troubling group dynamics. Research has demonstrated that the stress induced by crisis can handicap the ability to make good decisions and make the already existing risks of team dynamics on decision-making worse, as discussed earlier. For example, the dynamic required to fully assess the situation, to get the team to share the risks and consequences, and to come up with some viable options is extremely difficult to accomplish when the president is in the room. It is more likely that the CMT will be second-guessing what the president wants to happen as opposed to making solid recommendations.

Presidents need to juggle multiple critical priorities. Becoming all-consumed with a crisis can result in an inability to move forward on other, equally important strategic items. The best analogy is what could occur on a boat when someone catches a fish. If everyone runs to one side to see what happened, it is possible for the boat to capsize. The president needs to balance all the strategic priorities of the university, and in some instances, preoccupation with a crisis can inadvertently lead to strategic opportunities being missed or to another crisis.

Why, at the very point of crisis when leadership needs to be asserted the most, do I advocate that the president play a more circumscribed and defined role? Plenty of presidents have viewed a more hands-off approach as almost a dereliction of their duty, until they recognize that there is a better way—a way that still clearly protects and defines the role of leadership and the authority of the president.

Although it is difficult and requires a concerted effort, the president should take the following steps:

- Define the parameters of the president's role, including clear expectations regarding his or her level of engagement with the CMT and need for and frequency of information updates.
- Explicitly define the CMT as having the authority to act on behalf of the institution regarding the response to the crisis. That said, it must be clear which specific explicit decisions will be flagged and reserved for the president to make, as well as actions or recommendations that the president needs to review or needs to share with the board.
- Be able to step back—to actively give the CMT team some time and space to deliberate, discuss, and openly disagree as peers. The president should encourage the team to fully assess the risks and consequences of the event and come up with some viable options, along with expected outcomes, to help the president make the final decision when the time comes. This process is more effective if the president is not in the room.
- Identify a trusted lieutenant who can manage this process without the president being available: campus counsel, vice president of Business and Administration or the president's chief of staff are typically good choices, but selection of the CMT leader really requires internal discussion and agreement. The vice president of Communications may be too busy with communications-related tasks to easily serve in this capacity.

Rather than viewing the president as a solitary figure who alone has the insight and expertise to navigate through the crisis, recognize the importance of creating a trusted team that needs room, space, and time to juggle complex and competing priorities, in order to come to the table with specific recommendations and suggestions. The president is not abrogating his or her responsibility as the leader of the institution by taking a team approach but is instead giving the institution the best chance of success. At the end of the day, the president is going to need to make the hard decisions and take responsibility for them, but the less involved in the sausage-making, the more likely the president is to have a critical distance and broader perspective to decide whether the approach is appropriate.

Priority 3: Ensure a Stakeholder-Centric Approach to Decision-Making

The first two priorities define the management process and institutional capabilities that are important to have in place to prevent needlessly making the situation worse. What it does not inherently provide answers to are the core questions concerning an institution's values, or what is the "right" thing to do—which is why a stakeholder-centric approach to decision-making is so important.

A stakeholder-centric approach places a premium on understanding the perspective, the expectations, the needs and priorities of the range of stakeholders that are impacted by the institution's decisions: "What are our stakeholders expecting of us?" and "How do the decisions we need to make align with our core values as an institution?" This perspective reveals options and helps to ensure a proactive response. As examples time and time again have shown—from all schools in the Varsity Blues scandals or egregious and ongoing cases of sexual assault from MSU to USC—organizations frequently create long-term damage to their reputation and future when they are perceived as having

The Perils of a First-Time Presidency

Perhaps nothing tests a new president—and particularly if it is a first-time president—like a crisis within the first year in the role. The campus community still remembers the old president and how things used to be done; the board is hoping it made the right decision; and the new president is determined to make it to year two! All the typical challenges of a crisis—heightened scrutiny of decision-making, second-guessing by internal and external stakeholders—are exacerbated by the concern that as a new president, you had better not fail the first significant test of your leadership. Even closer to home, you will tend to view criticism of you as president as criticism of you as a person.

New presidents, in particular, need to watch out for:

- Overreacting to issues that can be appropriately managed by a direct report. It is easy to unnecessarily make an issue worse and potentially turn something into a crisis inadvertently.
- Prematurely "owning" the crisis as a way to demonstrate leadership and resolve, but instead undermining it.
- Becoming the "face" of the crisis, even if the underlying issues, particularly in a reputational crisis, may have predated your tenure.
- Overgeneralizing the importance or veracity of criticism and internalizing it as personal criticism; it may feel as if it's personal, but it can't be treated as such.

underreacted and not met the expectations of stakeholders during a time of crisis.

This approach stands in contrast to the normal operating mode of an institution in crisis, which is to focus primarily on meeting the institution's immediately achievable and short-term goals. The drivers of such a business-as-usual approach are the perceived internal constraints, culture and "office politics" inside the institution, which typically shape and limit the range of "acceptable" options. With a decision made, the focus of external engagement is less about understanding or meeting expectations than about positioning, explaining, or justifying decisions to stakeholders, whom the institution recognizes it needs to persuade and influence.

It is the role of the president to be sure that the CMT is aware of and is challenging its own assumptions about the appropriate response. Crisis management can fail spectacularly if decisions are based on business-as-usual thinking, leading to a significant disconnect between the decisions and actions the organization takes during a crisis and the expectations of stakeholders—the definition of reputational risk.

Priority 4: Understand the President's Role as the "Face" of the Institution

Standard crisis-management advice—as well as the natural inclination for most presidents—is to quickly and publicly take responsibility for the events and issues that occur on their campus. I disagree. This advice is really only suitable to crises in which there is a "victim"—natural disasters, active shooter, and the like. Indeed, it is not only appropriate but also relatively risk free for the president to reflect the anxieties felt on the campus—to demonstrate empathy, concern, and compassion, as well as a determination to move on, learn from the events, and emerge with an even stronger institution in these situations. However, these types of crisis reflect only about 10 percent of the total.

When facing the far more common "self-inflicted" crisis, it is absolutely essential that the president be protected and not immediately be established as the frontline communicator. This is not a suggestion designed to protect the presidency only; rather, it is meant to protect the reputation of the institution as well.

Beware of "Owning the Crisis"

An effective leader is someone who clearly takes responsibility but who does not micromanage every little thing that happens on

Protecting the President's Voice

Keep in mind that, to a large degree, value is created by scarcity. A president's voice can be more impactful when heard less frequently, and a president's time better appreciated when it is harder to win.

That said, there appears to be increasing pressure for presidents at many schools to comment on everything that occurs on campus and plenty of things that don't, but on which the presidential perspective is requested. This is particularly true in today's political climate, when presidents are asked for a statement on just about any political issue, from climate change and immigration policies to budget and racial tensions. While a president can face criticism for not speaking out on a topic, it is highly likely that by speaking, a president will face criticism about addressing issue X while remaining silent on issue Y. Presidents need to be far more circumspect about when they speak, in order to maintain the ability to have impact when it really matters. Criteria would include:

- Is there someone closer to the issue on campus who should express the institution's point of view, perhaps the vice president of Student Affairs or the provost?
- Is this an issue that has already been addressed proactively through policy or programs?

If the answer to these two questions is yes, there is no reason for the president to become engaged. If the answer is no, then the following question should be asked:

- Beyond generic words of support or reiteration of values, does the president have something important to say that is aligned with the strategy of the institution?

If the answer to the final question is yes, then the president should address the issue. If it is no, it is probably better to keep the presidential "powder" dry, to be used at a future, more important point in time.

campus. Unfortunately, the fastest way to "own" an issue is to be-come closely associated with it by becoming the spokesperson—whether that means actually speaking with reporters or being quoted in statements. While anathema to the way most presidents think about their role in significant issues or crisis, speaking too early in a crisis unnecessarily creates a number of problems:

Heightened interest. Having the president engage in an issue too early may give the issue or event more credence and importance than it makes sense to convey to the commu-nity, and this tactic could backfire. In self-inflicted crises, it is easy to increase interest and exacerbate risk by saying more than you need. Rather than conveying leadership, this response could elevate community concern that the situation is potentially worse than it actually is.

Lost opportunity to "escalate" later. Particularly in the early stages of a crisis, it is usually not clear what other "shoes might drop" or how the crisis might morph and change. Having someone closer to the issue—the athletic director, the vice president of Student Affairs, or whomever—serve as the initial member of the leadership team serving as spokesperson will give the president breathing room. If the president owns the issue from the outset, it is simply impossible for her or him to recede into the background as things develop. Media and other stakeholders will expect a continuing visible presence of the president. Creating an opportunity to escalate later preserves the president's ability to engage, should the situation further deteriorate. Particularly on small campuses, this may be difficult to do, as the president may regularly comment on all sorts of issues of far less importance, potentially leading to criticism that the president is somehow ducking the issue.

Damage to the president's leadership. Close association with the issue can lead to the president, personally and professionally, becoming indelibly marked and potentially damaged by the issue. If the president is clearly front and center, it's more likely that responsibility for any failures will be laid at his or her door.

If it is necessary for the president to visibly engage on the issue, a typically effective model is for the president to give the community a written statement clearly outlining/disclosing the facts and showing concern and a determination to resolve the underlying issue. A drip-drip-drip of disclosures is the equivalent of death by a thousand cuts, and the best course is to get all the facts, disclose them, address them, and move on. Included in this statement should be a clear delegation of ongoing management to a senior administrative member. By taking this route, the president has the opportunity to demonstrate leadership without getting caught in the inevitable back and forth that will ensue over the next several days, weeks, and possibly months.

Focus on Critical Stakeholders, Not the Media

Anxiety about the press can, unfortunately, become an overriding concern for any leader in a crisis. This is natural; one poor performance during a 20/20 interview can change the impression stakeholders have about a president's leadership for a long time to come. While understandable, this focus on media can be counterproductive.

Rather than thinking about how to deal with the press, a more effective communications strategy is to meet the expectations and information needs of the stakeholders most impacted by the crisis. If key stakeholders are satisfied—be they parents, students, alumni, trustees, faculty, accreditors, or the local community—with the substance, timing, and sequencing of information, it is far more likely that criticism will be muted. Keep in mind that with social media, every grievance can be amplified, and accusations of being more concerned with media relations than with faculty or student relations in almost every instance adds to risk and criticism.

Any decision regarding the president's role in media relations needs to be weighed against the other roles the president needs to play in broader stakeholder communications: coordinating with the board, leadership at the system office in a multicampus state system; making one-on-one calls with key alumni, donors, legislators, academic leaders, and others in the community; as well as serving as ambassador to those directly impacted by the issue or event. Direct engagement with these stakeholders—particularly when not designed as a "photo-op" but an opportunity for genuine engagement—can be highly effective, both in building support for the position taken by the administration and, tangentially, in the media optics of the response priorities.

A president absolutely can survive a crisis, but it takes clear leadership, decision-making aligned with an institution's values, meeting stakeholder expectations, an ability to manage multiple and sometimes opposing demands, and the establishment of a team that can "speak truth to power." By prioritizing the proactive approach to reputational risk management advocated throughout this book, a president has both a better chance of proactively preventing a crisis from occurring in the first place and responding effectively when it does. The reputational risk management maturity model described in the final chapter of this book is one way to gauge how ready the president, and the institution, is to effectively manage this key strategic risk.

Chapter 9

Frameworks and Models to Manage Reputational Risk

At the start of this book, I suggested that since reputational risk can often seem too broad and nebulous a concept, it can be difficult to decide what an institution of higher education should do to help ensure that it is has a capability sufficient to manage the risk. Hopefully, the preceding chapters have increased clarity concerning reputational risk and the necessary constituent capabilities, processes, and mindset to effectively manage it. In this final chapter, two new frameworks are introduced:

1. *The Culture and Capability Framework* highlights the degree to which an organization's culture, leadership style, and values either actively support or impede an ability to manage reputational risk.
2. *The Reputational Risk Maturity Model* is aligned with the reputational risk management model introduced in chapter 1. The maturity model provides an ability to assess an institution's current state of readiness to effectively manage reputational risk and defines pathways to improve and build capabilities over time.

Reputational Risk Culture and Capability Framework

As discussed throughout, the ability to manage reputational risk is, at a high level, the combination of two primary variables, capability and culture.

> *Capability* is the degree to which an organization is prepared and has optimized its process and ability to both respond to unexpected crisis events and to proactively identify and mitigate potentially corrosive issues—essentially, the effectiveness of its risk management, crisis management, and issues management capability combined.

> *Culture* is the degree to which the organization's culture, leadership, and strategy is based on a shared understanding of the values and expectations of the stakeholders on whom its ongoing and future success is reliant. The culture variable is therefore essentially stakeholder sensitivity—the degree to which reputational risk is reduced through alignment of stakeholder expectations with institutional decision-making.

With Capability shown on the x axis and Culture on the y axis, these two axes then create a two-by-two matrix and four theoretical quadrants, in which every institution can be placed, with the optimal position on the grid in the upper right-hand corner. Every organization can be assessed based on these two scales, which both reveal the degree of reputational risk as well as identify areas where there are opportunities to improve. Birds and their associated characteristics have been used to crystalize these concepts, as discussed in more detail below.

Ostrich Organizations: Heads in the Sand

Ostriches have some inherent advantages: they are large and they can run. However, they are also flightless, conspicuous, typically shy, and when faced with danger either run away or hide, apocryphally known for putting their heads in the sand. Ostrich

Characteristics:
Highly innovative with high stakeholder expectations, Peacocks can suffer from overconfidence due to previous success, resulting in insufficient preparedness. In addition, they often believe that "doing the right thing" is all that is needed to protect reputation.

Characteristics:
Proactive, risk-aware, and attuned to their environment, Hawks view reputation as a key asset and a fundamental input into decision-making. This approach can lead to a long-term, competitive advantage.

Characteristics:
Ostriches are unwilling to acknowledge risk or take meaningful steps to reduce it and are, therefore, often caught by surprise when there is a crisis. Additionally, low stakeholder awareness tends to exacerbate risk & undermines competitiveness.

Characteristics:
An emphasis on on preparation ensures that Robins have a solid risk-management approach. However, an insufficient understanding of reputational risk and/or issues management can leave them vulnerable.

CULTURE

CAPABILITY

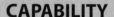

The Culture and Capability Framework

organizations can be large institutions with a strong position in their market, leading to complacency. They typically fail to identify strategic threats to their future or truly appreciate risk. If the threat or risk does materialize, ostriches either run or make a somewhat pointless attempt to hide.

Capability. Ostrich organizations either deliberately avoid or discount risk. An unwillingness to prepare or anticipate risk means that when something does happen the ostrich is caught flat-footed and surprised. Decisions made in a crisis will typically undermine, rather than enhance, the credibility of the organization and its leadership. Even if they recognize that there is a risk, ostrich organizations would prefer to not address it, and any activities are driven by a "check-the-box" compliance mindset as opposed to becoming part of the operating culture.

Culture. The ostrich organization will mistakenly believe that, because it is tall and has a relatively good viewpoint, it understands what its stakeholders expect. It suffers from confirmation bias, however, and is really only interested in engaging with those that like ostriches. The focus of external engagement is on explaining why the ostrich is right all along, with little to no interest in listening to the perspectives of stakeholders.

Example. Michigan State University and specifically its handling of the Larry Nasser scandal would be a good example of an ostrich organization. It failed to identify the risks and, even when presented with them, did not respond in a way that its stakeholders expected. The "head in the sand" approach exacerbated the impact to the organization, which could, quite conceivably, have responded in a way that would have strengthened its reputation and its leadership. It failed. Ostrich organizations are the least capable of managing reputational risk.

What to Do? Everything. Ostrich organizations are in an unsustainable position in today's highly scrutinized and hypercritical environment. Issues and crises are not unlikely "black swan" events for which it is impossible to prepare; rather, they are the new normal. It is only a matter of time before an issue

What about Black Swans?

What about one of the most frequently referenced birds when discussing crises—the "black swan"!? While the black swan is actually not that rare (it is the state bird of Western Australia), it was historically viewed as something that simply did not exist: all swans were white. The concept of the black swan to describe highly improbable events was popularized by Nassim Taleb's book of the same name.*

One of the key concepts of the book is essentially it is not worth the time spent trying to identify a black swan event but rather spend the energy on mitigating its potential impact—which in the context of this book would be build a capability and culture that can protect the institution against reputational risk, whatever its origin.

Unfortunately, the phrase "black swan" has become so popular that it is actually used to describe its exact opposite. COVID-19 has frequently been described as a black swan, despite the risk of an animal-to-human leap by a deadly virus having been identified as a key risk—one that has occurred multiple times in the recent past and that organizations and governments should have been prepared for.

While many things are described as black swans that obviously are not, the wake-up call to become more resilient and prepared has also become subverted: if black swan events are essentially highly improbable, unknowable, and unpredictable, what value is there in trying to prepare? Building a capability to effectively respond is vital—because it is the perception of the response that typically creates more reputational damage than the precipitating issue or crisis.

*Nassim Nicholas Taleb, *The Black Swan: The Impact of the Highly Improbable* (Random House, 2007).

or a crisis profoundly and detrimentally changes stakeholders' view of the institution.

Peacock Organizations: Pride before a Fall

Peacocks are admired for their beauty, are often associated with royalty, and in some religions symbolize immortality and regeneration. Their unique feather pattern and color ensure that the peacock will stand out from the crowd. Unfortunately, in addition to these qualities, the peacock is also associated with pride.

Peacock organizations are typically highly successful, and the leadership team can be showy, frequently highly innovative, unique, and setting new standards. They are also typically convinced that they are the proverbial "smartest guys in the room."[*]

Capability. Peacock organizations view themselves as almost immortal and not subject to the same risks and pitfalls as other, more mundane institutions, and so they fail to prepare or develop any capability to manage reputational risk. Despite events and evidence to the contrary, "Well, that could never happen to us" is the typical response. Denial might then be paired with overconfidence, which leads to a slow understanding of the risk the organization faces. Once faced with the inevitable, a reactive, inconsistent approach is most likely, often described as "too little, too late."

Culture. Peacock organizations have been given the benefit of the doubt over time, which builds an unwarranted confidence that can, in its worst form, turn to arrogance. While historically attuned to stakeholder expectations and generally successful, this track record can lead to dissonant voices or concerns being marginalized, and to early warning signs that "not everything is perfect" being ignored. Because these are often high-profile

---

[*]Bethany McLean and Peter Elkind, *The Smartest Guys in the Room* (Portfolio Trade, 2003), is a retelling of the Enron crisis, a compelling cautionary tale that captures the challenges of leadership in crisis and the complete disconnect between values and decision-making.

institutions, the reputational damage can be more significant, as the disconnect between stakeholder expectations and how the institution responds becomes huge.

Example. The University of Southern California and its handling of both the scandal involving the dean of Medicine as well as the follow-on handling of allegations of serial sexual assault by a gynecologist (for which, in early 2021 the institution settled claims exceeding $1 billion). Prior to these crises, USC had been on a transformative path, leaving the epithet "University of Spoiled Children" long behind. The remarkably successful tenure of its president, facilitated by the seemingly unquestioning trust of its board, led USC to believe it didn't need to take the accusations too seriously. Remarkably, not only did USC fail to learn anything from the example of Michigan State University, but widespread and long-held stakeholder dissatisfaction on a broad range of cultural and leadership issues led to the departure of the president, among other sweeping changes. The Varsity Blues scandal also centered on USC. With its fundamental values and ethics questioned, new leadership looks to repair USC's damaged reputation.

What to Do? Due to their high profile, peacock organizations have to start to anticipate and proactively manage issues that, left unaddressed, could cause serious reputational damage in a less-adoring environment. Likewise, it is important to recognize that peacocks will, at some point, have targets on their backs, and they need to get ready for the inevitable crisis. Peacocks will initially be given the benefit of the doubt in a crisis, owing to the success they've had in other areas, but if the response is viewed as ineffective, the trust and reputation built over the years will evaporate quickly.

Robin Organizations: A Stitch in Time Saves Nine

The quintessential early bird, robins are often seen focused on the ground, tugging at the occasional earthworm. They are industrious, alert to their immediate surroundings, and, in spite of their small size, comfortable in both urban and country settings. Robins (particularly English robins, compared to their larger and less cute American counterparts!) are popular because of their red breasts and generally amiable appearance and demeanor. Robins can also be a little bossy and can mistakenly believe that their red breast makes them somewhat intimidating.

Robin organizations tend to be well aware of the risks in their immediate environment and put an emphasis on being prepared. This attention generally allows robin organizations to stay out of the limelight. A belief that stakeholders already know they "do the right thing" is overemphasized, and little effort has been put toward building goodwill that could protect them in the future.

Capability. The approach is typically a prosaic focus on traditional risk management components—compliance, insurance, environmental, health and safety, and emergency response. More than a paper plan, there is a genuine capability to handle normal incidents—disruptions to operations, workplace violence, and so on. However, there is often little to no recognition of reputational risk or concept of how both to identify it or effectively manage it.

Culture. Robins are not as focused on understanding stakeholder opinion, preferring to focus on core competencies and let their track record speak for itself. With little to no profile, however, robins risk being defined by others, particularly on negative issues, and they can be significantly damaged by nontraditional risks.

Example. Examples of robin organizations are harder to identify, not just because of the seriousness with which they address risk management, but also because they are less likely to be subject to the criticism faced by other organization types, either due to willful avoidance (the ostrich) or arrogance (the peacock). That said, the vast majority of institutions of higher education fall into this "robin" category—not having given sufficient thought or defined processes to support effective management of reputational risk. Depending on the situation, leadership qualities and values of the organization, the line between a "robin" and an "ostrich" can sometimes be too fine—and once faced with a significant reputational risk for which the organization is not prepared, a head in the sand approach can be expected.

What to Do? Build on the discipline and rigor incorporated into your existing risk management programs and expand the frame to incorporate proactive issues management and a leadership capability and process to successfully manage response to nonphysical, reputational risks. Recognize that reputation is too important to be left unmanaged.

Hawk Organizations

Hawks are small birds of prey that can detect not just visible light but ultraviolet light and even magnetic fields. This acuity, together with the ability to fly high, gives hawks an unmatched perspective and viewpoint on the environment they inhabit. Effective hunters, hawks are also risk-aware, building strong nests and locating them in high and hard to disturb locations, recognizing that they are still relatively small birds.

Hawk organizations are typically well prepared and are unlikely to be caught off guard. Their perspective, experience, and vision mean that hawks not only manage the specific challenge at hand but also focus on anticipating potential impacts and consequences of issues and events.

Capability. A hawk organization recognizes that its relatively strong position comes from constant vigilance; hawks are constantly surveying the horizon and are risk-aware, able to anticipate issues and prevent themselves from escalating into crises. When a crisis is unavoidable, the hawk is prepared, trained, and fully capable of protecting itself.

Culture. Hawks have to work particularly hard to reassure skeptical stakeholders about their intentions. Despite the difficulties, hawk organizations attempt to take every opportunity to demonstrate good intentions, values, and commitment to engage meaningfully, even with those naturally opposed to them.

Example. Fortunately, there are actually many examples of universities and colleges clearly exhibiting hawklike characteristics, even if that is apparent to stakeholders only on specific issues. Georgetown's reconciliation and memorialization regarding its history with slavery, Middlebury's approach to divesting from fossil fuels, or UC Berkeley's handling of freedom of speech issues are good examples of hawk response. As the birthplace of the Free Speech Movement, this issue has always been core to UC Berkeley's fundamental values. The university knows what it stands for and is fully aware, prepared, trained, and capable of ensuring safety on campus while protecting free speech rights—despite having equally important commitments to supporting racial equity and diversity, values often under attack by right-wing speakers.

What to Do? Don't let the absence of a crisis lull an institution into a false sense of security or, conversely, make it second-guess whether this capability is needed in the first place. Lack of a crisis or a significant issue is proof that proactive strategies to reduce reputational risk are working, not that there is no risk to start with. Without an actual crisis, continued program refinement, effective governance, and regularly exercising the Crisis Management Team are the only ways to prevent a gradual deterioration in those capabilities important for survival.

This two-by-two matrix is intended to be a lighthearted way of considering different institutional cultures and their impact on a willingness and ability to manage the challenge of reputational risk. The underlying point is actually serious—the lack of recognition most institutions have about what quadrant they are actually in! An ostrich or a peacock organization, for example, is unlikely to ever recognize in the first place that they need to become more like a hawk—in fact, they either think they already are a hawk (a peacock view) or they think the whole concept is rubbish and not worth their time (an ostrich view). Likewise, the robin often mistakenly thinks it shares hawk-like attributes—until it is faced with an existential issue for which it is hopelessly unprepared.

Even if there is a recognition of gaps in capability or a culture that is insensitive to reputational risk, most organizations find it hard to change. There is typically only one exception: a crisis. When the inevitable crisis occurs, the response by the institution compounds the damage to its reputation, standing, and ongoing viability, which then requires it to completely reevaluate the type of institution it really is and needs to be in the future. A "change at the top" is a frequent way to signal to stakeholders that, going forward, things will be different.

The call to action in this book is to essentially change that dynamic—to not wait until a crisis has overwhelmed an organization before acting; to recognize that in the higher education marketplace today, reputational risk is significant. The second model—the reputational risk capability maturity model—provides a roadmap to actually build this capability.

Reputational Risk Management Maturity Model

The concept of a capability maturity model was developed by Carnegie Mellon University in 2006,* and while initially developed to improve software development, it has subsequently been incorporated into many fields. It is a way to assess the current effectiveness of a capability and define what needs to be in place to improve performance. This approach can be applied, therefore, to how to steadily increase an institution's capability to manage reputational risk. This maturity model is based on the reputational risk management framework introduced in chapter 1, which essentially aligns the three components of risk management, crisis management, and issues management, which, when combined, constitute a holistic approach to managing reputational risk.

Risk management represents an organization's foundational approach, typically driven by nonreputational drivers, such as

*See https://en.wikipedia.org/wiki/Capability_Maturity_Model.

	① INITIAL	② INCONSISTENT	③ DEFINED	④ PROACTIVELY MANAGED	⑤ OPTIMIZED
...AN ...BILITY	Basic Clery Act & Emergency Response Plans, crisis response undocumented, ad hoc	"Paper" plans for Crisis Communications or Crisis Management, siloed response	Clear, aligned Crisis Management, Communications & Emergency Plans	Integrated planning; response capability understood & aligned	Reputational Risk Management embedded as part of organizational culture • driver of preparedness, strategy, and decision-making • enables rapid understanding of complex problems • innovative, provides competitive edge • fully aligned teams, a true "capability" • recognized by board as being critical to stewardship
...NING & ...RENESS	Isolated awareness	Limited awareness of plans, responsibilities; inconsistently used and/or tested	Predictable training cycle with focus on increasing familiarity and capability	High familiarity, teams tested in challenging, realistic scenarios	
...ENSING	Limited risk-specific reporting procedures (e.g., ethics "hotline," Title IX)	Reactive, informal incident reporting/escalation procedures in place	Reporting & screening process established; preliminary issues identification & management	Key Risk Indicators actively used, culture supports sharing "bad news"	
...NANCE	No clear ownership	Compliance-driven, project-based budget	Accountability, policies defining expectations, allocated budget	Managed program with accompanying goals/metrics supported by appropriate budget	

The Reputational Risk Maturity Model

legal or regulatory requirements, and is part of normal operations. Examples include effective compliance programs to ensure that policies to broadly reduce risk are followed; and emergency response plans to protect and respond to events that threaten the life or safety on the campus.

Crisis management represents an organization's leadership and strategic capability to effectively respond to and mitigate the risks associated with significant, nonphysical events and issues, as well as the impacts and consequences of sudden, unexpected physical events. Crisis management can mitigate reputational risk by demonstrating a clear capability aligned with the institution's values, a sensitivity to stakeholder concerns, and done well can burnish reputation despite a significant crisis or issue occurring.

Issues management represents the most advanced and sophisticated component of an approach to reduce reputational risk. Potential issues of strategic concern are identified in advance, plans put in place to course-correct the organization's approach or to strengthen understanding and support among important stakeholders of the institution's position. Issues management can proactively reduce reputational risk and create a reservoir of good will among stakeholders critical for the institution's long-term success.

In common with all capability maturity models, the ability to manage reputational risk is assessed against five levels of maturity:

Level 1. *Initial:* chaotic and ad hoc, the starting point for a new or undocumented process.

Level 2. *Inconsistent:* the process is documented but inconsistently used or understood.

Level 3. *Defined:* the process is part of standard operational procedures, is aligned, and essentially is fit for purpose.

Level 4. *Proactively Managed:* agreed-upon standards, metrics, funding, and governance support a genuine capability.

Level 5. *Optimized:* is innovative, provides a competitive edge, and is fundamental to organizational values.

These are the five levels to a mature capability to manage—essentially—anything. The reputational risk management capability maturity model introduced here maps four variables against which progress on this scale can be measured.

Risk Sensing

Risk sensing is a broad category that addresses two important capabilities discussed at length earlier: (1) the incident reporting and screening process required to assess the relative importance of an issue or event that has occurred on campus in order to deploy the appropriate resources, expertise, and level of authority; and (2) the proactive issues management process of identifying potential issues that could, over time, impact the reputation of the institution.

Level 1 (Initial) means that there are limited, risk-specific reporting procedures in place, typically mandated by law or regulation.

Title IX reporting processes would be a good example, in place at almost every institution; or the establishment of ethics hotlines for staff and faculty to report troubling behavior anonymously. This level also includes basic compliance with Clery Act requirements notifying the community about threats to safety and aggregating that data annually to provide some sense of crime and safety issues on a specific campus. These reporting channels, however, typically end at either Human Resources or Legal or the Title IX Office and result in specific types of response or investigation. Level 1 also means that there is no issues management program in place, as well as an ad hoc and probably unpersuasive response to issues when they do occur.

Level 2 (Inconsistent) means that there is an ad hoc and informal processes to share and escalate bad news. While the range of risks will necessarily be broader than those captured by the channels noted above, the likelihood of an issue or event being reported is determined by an individual's willingness to do something beyond what would be expected—an exception rather than the rule. At level 2, even if an issue or event was escalated, the likelihood of an appropriate administrative response would be low, likewise driven by personal ethics or values as opposed to institutional culture. As a result, issues tend to fester unaddressed, bad news is not shared for fear of a "shoot the messenger" response, and the institution only identifies the issue once it is too late to prevent significant reputational damage—the perception of a cultural failing compounding the underlying risk. For proactive issues management, little is in place except for reactive processes related to crises that have already occurred, described earlier as the "barn door closing" strategy for issues management, or "too little too late."

Level 3 (Defined) means that conscious steps have been taken to develop a process and a culture that support the escalation of bad news, designed to counteract the natural human tendency to want not to report issues or events—either out of self-preservation or self-doubt—which means that the information can't possibly be accurate, or someone else would already have addressed it. At lower levels in the organization, it means managers being trusted by staff (or deans being trusted by faculty) to share issues of concern. At the dean and equivalent level across the institution, it means knowing exactly when and to whom to report issues, trends, or concerns, so that appropriate support and guidance can be provided. This enables the administration to analyze the issue or event, put it in context with other events occurring on campus, and juxtapose it against strategic priorities in order to decide how or if the institution needs to more broadly respond.

As with the crisis management capability, level 3 represents a significant jump in capability from level 2. The institution is far more sensitive about key stakeholders, has prioritized the relative importance of stakeholders on the institution, and has recognized the need for a concerted effort to proactively identify issues that could, over the next twelve months, impact the reputation of the institution if not addressed. In specific priority issue areas, cross-functional teams are in place to address identified gaps and remedies to close them, metrics are in place, and the institution is able to communicate clearly about its values, its approach, and its progress. Even if an incident does occur in this issue area, basic processes are clearly in place and demonstrated focus on improvement will reduce reputational damage.

Level 4 (Proactively Managed) refers to a culture and capability at an institution that is highly attuned to stakeholder expectations, has a clear process to report and escalate issues or events that could create reputational risk to the institution, and fundamentally has a culture that creates a dynamic that is the opposite of level 2: failing to raise issues of concern would be the exception to the rule, rather than vice versa. With information flow uninhibited, the administrative challenge is to have a process in place that appropriately analyzes and assesses the relative importance and potential impact of different events. It needs to be calibrated to ensure the administration doesn't become numb to all the problems and underreact or, conversely, consistently overreact, which can create its own set of problems and undermine the credibility of leadership. Risk sensing, however, refers to that ability to sense, to analyze, to assess—and at level 4, this process is clear, proactively managed, and assures that the organization is able to connect the dots between seemingly unrelated events.

Issues management programs are robust and proactively managed; issue owners are clearly identified, and the performance evaluations for issue owners incorporate progress against metrics; senior leadership regularly participates in issues-specific scenario-based discussions; and overall issue prioritization is reviewed at least annually to reflect strategic direction of the school, broader institutional and national context, and opportunities to strengthen institutional reputation among key stakeholders.

Plan Viability

Plan viability defines the degree to which there is a documented, repeatable process and capability to manage reputational risk, however it materializes. Aligned plans are necessary to define the process, but plans themselves are not sufficient to develop a true capability. Likewise, capability is not possible if it relies on individual expertise and judgment alone. If X happens, the response by the institution should result in Y. If the exact same thing occurs again, X happens and the outcome is B, sometimes W, and sometimes 12, the process (or lack of understanding of the process) has introduced variability, inconsistency, and therefore unnecessary additional risk.

Level 1 (Initial) means that basic expectations around safety and security are in place, essentially compliant with regulatory minimum requirements, such as the Clery Act, and that some components of basic emergency response are in place, for example, procedures to evacuate a building in case of a fire. Little is documented; rather, the capability, to the extent there is one, relies on individual experience.

Level 2 (Inconsistent) means that the institution has developed some of the initial phases of a crisis management capability, but they are often risk-specific, "operational" plans. One frequent example is the IT department's developing a cyber-response plan that either doesn't align with or define a crisis team and typically blends the operational and strategic response components. Another example of level 2 plan viability would be the development of a crisis communications plan. The communications team is often on the front end of poorly managed crises and starts to develop its own plan. This approach typically leads to a hybrid plan, which, in addition to capturing some components of crisis management, primarily focuses on communications—cataloging already used or approved messaging around key issues; identifying spokespeople who are trained and able to address specific issues; coordinating procedures between different communicators in decentralized organizations. Even if documented plans are in place, at level 2 they are insufficiently understood by those who need to use them to enable an effective response.

Level 3 (Defined) means that emergency management, crisis management, and crisis communications plans are properly aligned and defined, each with distinct roles and responsibilities, each able to work independently when that is all that is required, or in tandem when the event or issue requires clear coordination and multiple levels of response and decision-making. Essentially, the operational, communications, and strategic roles of different teams are defined, clear, documented, and understood by those who need to implement them. The ability to get to level 3 requires an institution-wide effort to break down inevitable "ownership" issues between what otherwise will remain siloed and disconnected response plans. At level 3, risk management and crisis management components of the framework are effectively aligned.

Level 4 (Proactively Managed) means that issues management components are incorporated into overall planning capability in a number of ways. First, priority issues identified as part of the issues management program are specifically linked into reporting and escalation criteria in response plans. Second, there are proactive issue-specific plans in place. In addition to aligning issues management and crisis management, the institution has moved from a place of defined "plans" to a defined "capability"— plans actually work, response is effective, and continuing improvement procedures are in place to ensure that the capability remains evergreen. Level 4 typically requires active engagement in post-incident reviews to learn from the issue or event that occurred. This happens by incorporating longer-term recovery strategies into the issues management program and, operationally, by learning what internal process or technology barriers impeded effective response.

While it is sad to say, many institutions are somewhere between a level 1 and a level 2 on the reputational risk maturity model. Some institutions have very defined emergency management programs, which can lead them to believe they are at a level 3 or level 4 capability, which would be the case if this were a narrower emergency management maturity model. However, it is not.

As has been addressed, reputational risks are far broader, more common, and frequently more impactful to an institution's reputation than is an "emergency." As a result, most schools are struggling at around a level 2—inconsistent—level of maturity, which explains why most schools are not effective at managing reputational risk.

Training and Awareness

Training and awareness and plan viability go hand in hand. Without viable and aligned plans, an institution's response is not going to be up to the task; without clear understanding of those plans, an institution is not going to have an actual capability but rather just documents—however useful—that just gather dust on a shelf.

Level 1 (Initial) means that training and awareness is isolated to specific pockets of the university campus, typically members of the Department of Public Safety or the university's own police force. Even within these pockets, awareness is low, and oftentimes formal training and exercising have not been conducted in years.

Level 2 (Inconsistent) represents broader, albeit limited awareness of plans. Training of a cross-functional Emergency Management Team may take place on a periodic basis, and on occasion university leadership may also be engaged but have a highly limited role. In fact, at many institutions, the EMT views the role of senior administrators in exercises as unnecessary, as training is focused entirely on operational response to physical issues (active shooter, natural disaster). Some other components of response may also take place, for example, media training, but this is rarely explicitly linked to broader crisis management. Facilitated tabletop exercises are the appropriate mode to increase awareness, identify gaps, and start to build capability.

Level 3 (Defined) means the institution has recognized that training and exercising are core components of building capability to respond to crises effectively. They should occur across all team levels and address the full range of risks, not just physical events. At Level 3, training includes on-boarding all new team members and conducting "refresher" training for the remainder, with a specific focus on what may have changed in plans, either due to improvements in technology or "lessons learned" in previous activations. Exercising is likewise predictable (typically annually, although there are many reasons, particularly at the leadership level, to hold focused, quarterly exercises), they address a full spectrum of reputational risk issues and are increasingly challenging and complex.

Level 4 (Proactively Managed) means that there is a strategic program plan in place that defines the level of capability expected of the organization and identifies and maps out key actions, discreet steps, and critical milestones required to build and maintain this capability. Part of a strategic program plan should be a clearly laid out series of progressively more challenging and complex exercises. The program plan is also aligned with the issues management program, so that response to crises created by priority issues is tested, validated, and folded back into the strategic approach to the issue.

The level of engagement and participation in all exercises is high, including at the executive level, as there is a recognition of the strategic and competitive value exercises can play in strengthening the institution's overall capability to manage reputational risk. At an exercising level, teams are capable of effectively responding, collaborating, and proactively identifying and managing the strategic impacts and consequences of the crisis in complex functional or full-scale exercises. While an actual crisis will always be challenging, institutional crisis "muscle memory" and defined processes will ensure that the response is proactive, will protect the institution's reputation, and will not inadvertently compound the impact of the underlying event.

Governance

Governance defines clear accountability, defined metrics, and program goals supported by allocated resources (budget, personnel, time) and clear reporting. In many organizations, governance trails the capability developed in other areas of the program, but it is clearly recognized as critical to establishing a viable, long-term culture and capability.

Level 1 (Initial) reflects the general lack of definition around who "owns" reputational risk and who, therefore, should be responsible for managing it. At the initial capability level, specific program components (e.g., emergency response) may be managed by the police or public safety officers, but broader governance is absent. There is little recognition of reputational risk beyond general lip service.

Level 2 (Inconsistent) means there is still no institutional ownership of reputational risk, and any efforts to address component parts are ad hoc, unbudgeted, and project-based: one-off attempts to solve a specific issue or risk that do little to build a broader capability institution-wide. Plans, to the extent they exist, are siloed and not aligned. At this level, typically there remains lack of clarity over what, if anything, can be done to manage reputational risk, which is frequently reduced to a "communications" problem.

Level 3 (Defined) reflects a recognition that reputational risk is a distinct, manageable risk (as opposed to a derivative risk, which can be solved, for example, through better operational controls). Program components are codified, formalized, and aligned. Not reactive and project-specific, there is a consistent programmatic budget, which will support the program as it evolves and matures over time, and clear leadership expectations.

Level 4 (Proactively Managed) typically means that the program is so integral that a clear policy is in place against which the program is managed and audited against specific expectations and standards. At this point, the approach is embedded as part of the culture of the organization. Metrics are in place at the issue level, the institutional level, and the program management level. Activity-based metrics are helpful from a program management perspective and essentially measure *input*—what level of effort and commitment is being made to support the program. As discussed earlier, better metrics for understanding the effectiveness of the reputational risk management program are the metrics that measure *output*—what difference has the program actually made.

Reaching Level 5 (Optimized). In the descriptions of levels 1-4, criteria for level 5 were not addressed. The reason is simple: level 5 requires that all areas—risk sensing, plan viability, training, and governance—be in place, because they are all mutually supportive. By the time level 5 has been achieved, this reputational risk management framework is embedded in the fabric of the institution and is perceived as giving the school a critical strategic advantage:

- Fully aligned and truly capable teams are able to manage effectively any issue or crisis that occurs on campus. Given that the effectiveness of response is the primary factor in the reputational damage the underlying event or issue can cause, this means that even crises present an opportunity to succeed and to differentiate from competition.

- A proactive issues management program enables the university to anticipate and mitigate the risks that other schools still face; substantively, the institution has the support and engagement of the stakeholders critical to its success.

- Even in the euphemistic "black swan" crisis, the process and mindset to rapidly distill complex problems and analyze competing strategic responses and their impacts are in place, thereby protecting the institution.

- The Board of Trustees has confidence in leadership's ability to effectively manage reputational risk. Moreover, the board views the program as a critical component of the broader, long-term stewardship of the institution, on a par with the importance and responsibility of maintaining financial stability. The board insists on regular reporting, at least annually, on reputational risk, and emerging reputational risks are systematically discussed, including the institution's approach to dealing with them.

Most universities, however, are at level 2 capability in terms of the reputational risk management framework, and frequently they languish there for some time; the significant capability gap between level 2 and level 3 requires an organizational commitment that is often difficult to achieve. Once level 3 has been achieved however, the value of the approach becomes obvious (crises are avoided, events are handled more effectively than in the past, leadership is able to focus on strategic opportunities as opposed to constantly fighting fires) that moving to advanced levels of capability is decreasingly difficult. Looking at the model and assessing where the institution's current capability exists, however, is a worthwhile effort and can help clarify areas of additional focus that will, over time, increase an institution's ability to proactively manage reputational risk.

Lies, Damn Lies, and Statistics: What Metrics Exist to Measure Reputational Risk?

Thus far I have discussed the importance of clearly defined metrics to measure the effectiveness of a proactive reputational risk management program, but that can be difficult to define at an institutional level, albeit easier at an issue-specific level (see chapter 7, which addressed issues management. But some work has been done, focused on large publicly traded companies, that is somewhat informative and at least interesting in terms of scaling the potential reputational damage caused by a poorly handled issue or crisis.

Stock Price

Some studies have suggested that there is a correlation between a company's stock price and the degree to which the company is perceived to have responded effectively to a crisis.* The difference between the direct, actual financial cost of the incident—a combination of additional costs and lost revenue—and the stock market's perception of the value of the company can be thought of as the "reputational damage" associated with the crisis.

This intuitively makes sense, and experience over many years shows a major decline in share price at key moments in high-profile corporate crises: Boeing and its reactions to two crashes of its newest plane, the 737Max; Volkswagen and the scandal regarding its cover-up of diesel engine performance against environmental goals; BP and its response to the Gulf oil spill; Sony and its data breach related to North Korea, and what it revealed about its internal corporate culture; and so on. Apart from making the case that poor response to crisis is not something that

---

Oxford Metrica/AON—"Reputation Review, 2011,"* http://www.oxfordmetrica .com/public/CMS/Files/825/Aon_Oxford%20Metrica%20Reputation%20Review _2011.pdf. This study did attempt to quantify share price.

higher education has a monopoly over, the challenge, of course, for higher education, is that there is no equivalent metric to stock price. Markets also move both up and down for reasons completely unrelated to an individual company's performance. It is at best an imperfect indicator.

Insurance Models

Some leading insurance and reinsurance companies have been grappling with how to insure reputational risk for a number of years, in order to sell an insurance product that would offset the financial loss of a significant "reputational event." Most solutions focus on an easily controllable metric: lost sales. If an event happens, and there has been a measurable decline in sales and—importantly—an ability to determine with some confidence *causality*, then an insurance product would reimburse for the lost sales, that is, the reputational damage.

Conversely, if an event happens (for example, leadership is involved in an accounting or sex scandal), but sales continued to hit targets, and in all other respects the event did not impact the ability of the corporation to generate revenue, then there was no impact from the event and thus no reputational loss. Whatever the event, it was unfortunate but essentially did not matter.

The fact that the insurance industry—which has a history of using data to develop all sorts of insurance products for every conceivable risk—has struggled to develop a reputational risk product in the same way it has developed a cyber risk product or business interruption insurance for physical events, speaks to the complexity with developing data to analyze reputation.

Potential Metrics for Higher Education

Viable metrics that could be used to calculate actual impact of a reputational event in higher education could include a combination of those shown below. The data also needs to match the length of the reputational impact, which can often be years. As a result, the data should reflect the broad range of indirect costs that an institution may occur over the longer term:

- Decline in first year enrollment and decrease in broader retention rates
- Increase in the tuition discount rate, to continue to attract the number of students required
- Increase in salary and benefits, to recruit key academics and researchers, and general increased time and resources required to recruit the talent the institution requires
- Decrease in research or partnership opportunities
- Increased accreditation and legislative scrutiny on all aspects of the institution's management and culture
- Decline in alumni giving (as a percentage of base and total dollar contributions)
- Increased costs associated with strengthened compliance programs
- Increased marketing costs, if applicable, when a component of the recovery strategy from the crisis event

These financial metrics are separate from short-term costs, such as costs associated with legal counsel and crisis consulting support, settlement costs, and so on. This is not to say these numbers are perfect—an institution dealing with multiple issues at the same time (an athletics crisis and racial incidents or a high-profile student death) would make it impossible to determine which of those crises had the most severe impact. This is another reason why issue-specific metrics can provide nuance and supplement inherently broader institutional-level metrics.

There are two additional challenges. The first is that these metrics are limited and are all essentially financial metrics— what quantifiable ways did the issue or crisis impact our financial strength? Broader metrics can be deployed that test stakeholder perception of the institution and how it has changed as a result of the (mis)handling of the issue or crisis. Do stakeholders trust the institution? And its leadership? Does it reflect their values? Was it open and ethical in the way decisions were made and information communicated? As discussed in the section on issues management, this type of stakeholder research is rarely, if ever, done by most universities, and its real value is when this kind of "pulse" survey is conducted regularly over time.

The second challenge is that these metrics measure the financial impact of an event or issue after it has happened. They are all essentially trailing indicators—metrics to calculate how bad the reputational damage was from the issue or event—as opposed to leading indicators. While valuable and an important way to measure post-crisis recovery, these metrics aren't helpful if the primary goal of a proactive reputational risk management program is to prevent issues and crisis from occurring in the first place. The issue-specific metrics should be helpful in this regard, together with the proactive tools discussed earlier, such as the crisis planning case, and the asset impairment valuation model.

What's Past Doesn't Have to Be Prologue

"What's past is prologue" is generally true (from Shakespeare's aptly named *The Tempest*), but it doesn't have to be. Newspaper headlines will continue to be filled with stories of abysmal failure of response to issues and crises—but hopefully, those stories will be viewed as not the inevitable outcome of a crisis but as a wake-up call (if one were still needed) that there has to be a better way.

Certainly, the environment in which universities operate is unlikely to get any easier; in fact, it is safe to assume it will become even more complex and more challenging. Technology is not going to slow down or make crisis response any easier; budget pressures, new models of delivering higher education, and changing demographics are going to make the underlying economics of higher education as a sector harder; contentious political and social issues—while always changing—will continue to be revealed first in campuses across the country.

Learning and improving is the absolute minimum expectation we have of students—and every institution of higher education likewise needs to learn the lessons and improve its approach to managing reputational risk. It's the minimum required if an institution is going to survive, let alone thrive, in this complex and competitive environment. Unlike crises, this improvement will go unheralded, and it will not be the subject of headlines. But there will be a quiet appreciation that will strengthen the ties that bind key stakeholders to the institution they love.

Index

Page numbers in **bold** refer to tables.

crisis (*continued*)
36-37; predictability of impact of, 73, 74-75; preparation for, 122; resolution of, 78; response to, 25-26, 152; self-inflicted, 122-23, 137; stakeholders and media, 78; things that can go wrong in, 26-41

crisis communication: branding campaigns, 82; calendar of events and, 90; consistent messaging, 86, 88-89; contradictions and errors, 88; core competencies of, 82; *vs.* crisis management, 20; critical role of, 80-81, 104; *vs.* emergency communications, 86; evolution of, 82; "hard Q&As," 90-91; hidden domains, 97; leadership in, 82; media-centric approach, 83, 91, 167; *vs.* media relations, 81, 83, 86; microsites and, 93; multiple levels of, 86, 88; "newsroom" model, 82; "not communicate" approach, 94-97; ongoing investigations approach, 96-97; operational function, 82; planning, 89, 158; president role in, 135-40; protection of reputation and, 83; rapid response capability, 101-2; shared messaging, 90; social media and, 91, 98-99, 101-4; stakeholder-centric approach, 83, 84-85, 89, 92-94, 124, 140-41; strategy in, 89, 90, 94, 96, 97

Crisis Communications Team, 35, 54, 89-90

crisis management: ad hoc approach to, 33; bad news sharing, 130, 132; bifurcation of process of, 38; Board of Trustees and, 124, 127-30; business-as-usual thinking and, 137; challenges of, 26-41, 68; chaos as operating mode in, 33-34; components of effective, 15, 41, 77, 80, 89, 104; context of, 47-49; *vs.* crisis communication, 20; decision-making and, 56, 67, 73; definition of, 17, 19, 21, 53, 153; *vs.* emergency management, 19-20, 54-56, 58-59; escalation process, 43; evolution of, 52, 167-68; faculty's role in, 125-27; goal of, 26; implementation challenges, 51-52, 79; importance of clarity in, 54; inherently inconsistent approach to, 33; leadership playbook for, 32-33, 122-23; legal framework, 37; "Lessons Learned" procedures, 168; media coverage of, 167; over- and underreaction in, 135-36; over-optimism in, 28; "ownership" issues, 137, 139, 158; paper CMT and, 35; in peacock organizations, 148; as perishable skill, 79; planning, 60, 67, 68-69, 158; pre-emptive measures, 42-43; president's role in, 123-24, 126-27, 130, 132-35; priorities of, 130; reactive *vs.* proactive approach, 75; reporting process, 43-45; response structure, 33, 59-60; risk assessment, 49-51; screening process, 43, 52; "shoot the messenger" tendency, 132; spokesperson in, 139; stakeholder relationships and, 124, 140-41; studies of, vii; teams' roles and responsibilities, 15, 31-32, 43, 60-64, 134, 135; technology and, 167; "too little, too late" outcome, 33; written statement, 140; *vs.* zero-sum game, 26

Crisis Management Team (CMT): activation of, 43, 45, 51, 52; authority of, 60, 64-65, 90, 134; backup team members, 65; Board of Trustees and, 129-30; closeout procedures, 78-79; communications strategy and, 90; coordinator of, 64, 72; crisis management and, 66, 134; decision-making process, 65, 67, 75-78, 133; effectiveness of, 32, 36; extended members, 63; issues management and, 118; leader of, 62, 63-64, 72; legal advice, 36; "Lessons Learned" procedures, 79; members of, 49, 62-63; operation problems, 67-68; paper, 35; presidents' engagement with, 134; roles and responsibilities of, 33-34, 36, 49-50, 53-54, 60, 62, 63-64, 112; scribe of, 62, 64; strategic priorities of, 56; structure of, 62; war rooms, 34

Crisis Management Team meetings: identification of impacts and consequences, 72-73; in-between meetings, 71-72; information sharing, 70; leadership of, 70; length of, 69; planning case, 74-75; progress report, 70; recap and next steps, 71; schedule, 71; situation update, 69-70; strategic discussion, 70-71; structure of, 72; typical problems of, 69

culture and capability framework, 143-45, 147, 149, 150-52, 154

cyber-response plan, 158

cyber security IT infrastructure, 106

data breach impact, 117

Data Breach Response Team, 51

decision-making: Board of Trustees' involvement in, 128-29; crisis-induced stress and, 28, 29; instinct and intuition, 76; leadership and, 30-31; options analysis tool, 76-77; president's role in, 30-31, 133; stakeholder-centric approach to, 84-85, 105, 124, 135-37; value judgment, 39-41, 76

Department of Homeland Security, 55

diversity issues, 119

Edelman Trust Barometer, 9

Eisenhower, Dwight D., 69

Elkind, Peter, 147

email systems, 92

emergency communications, 86, 87

emergency management: *vs.* crisis management, 54-56, 58-59; definition of, 19-20; operating model for, 56; priorities of, 55

Emergency Management Plan, 31, 158

Emergency Management Team, 52, 160

Emergency Operations Center (EOC), 31, 56, 132

Emergency Operations Team, 49, 54, 55, 56, 70

emergency response: *vs.* crisis response, 16

Emergency Response Team, 35

Enron crisis, 147

enterprise risk management, 16

events: "black swan," 145, 146; crisis communications for, 86; impact of, 20, 117-18; importance of calendar of, 90; non-crisis-related, 48; physical, 19, 31, 43, 55, 137, 153, 165; reporting of, 44, 45, 50, 156; screening process, 42-43, 52

Executive Leadership Team (ELT), 32
Executive Policy Group (EPG), 31, 55
"eyes wide open" approach, 76, 114

faculty: credibility of, 125; crisis management and, 125-27; factions within, 126; institutional reputation and, 125; power over cooperation, 125; president and, 126-27, 130; resistance to change, 125; tenure of, 125-26
Faculty Senate, 124, 126
fake news, 9
Ford, Henry, 105
Franklin, Benjamin, 11
Freedom of Information Act (FOIA), 39, 98
freedom of speech, 40, 57, 151

governance, 161-63
groupthink, 28, 29-30
Grove, Andy: *Only the Paranoid Survive*, 46

hate speech, 108
hawk organizations, 144, 150-52
health care crisis response, 20
hidden domains, 97, 98
higher education: challenges of, 3, 4; crisis management and, 20; metrics for, 165-67; reputational risks, 8, 10-11, 165-66; stakeholder relationships, 2; trust deficit in, 10

impaired asset model, 116-17, 119, 167
Incident Command System (ICS), 54-55
incident reporting and screening process, 45-48, 49-51, 101, 154

Incident Response Team, 51
incidents, 22, 23
institutions: fragmentation of, 3-4; operating mode during crisis, 136
issues: assumptions about, 117-18; components of, 107; cost of "solving," 113-14; *vs.* crisis, 19, 22, 108, 120; definition of, 23, 106; identification and mitigation of, 105-6, 109-12; impact of, 48, 73, 167; "industry," 108; initial list of potential, 110-11; metrics, 110, 118-19; monitoring of, 49-50; ownership of, 118; prioritization of, 111-12; reporting and escalation of, 50; response options to, 49-51, 108; slow-moving, 107; societal, 108
issues management: accept strategy, 113-14; accountability in, 119; build strategy, 114-15; change strategy, 113; danger of inaction in, 107; definition of, 15, 21-22, 111, 153-54; educate strategy, 115-16; financing modeling in, 116-18; institutional culture and, 121; leadership in, 109, 112, 118; methodology of, 105-6; objective of, 112; options analysis and decision-making, 111, 112-17; ownership and metric assignment, 111, 118-20; proactive, 154, 158-59; programs, 157; reactive nature of, 106; reporting process, 118; reputational research, 110; stakeholder engagement, 111, 120-21; time and, 107-8
Issues Management Council (IMC), 118
issues-to-crisis continuum, 22-24

Johari Window, 95

Katehi, Linda, 100
Kent State Massacre, 57-58
Kissinger, Henry, vii, 66

Larry Nassar scandal, 37, 145
leadership: confidence in, 128, 129; decision-making and, 30-31; reputational risk and, 24
leadership teams. *See* Crisis Management Team (CMT)
legal advice: *vs.* advice from an attorney, 39
Loh, Wallace, 122

Managing Crises before They Happen (Mitroff), 95
McLean, Bethany, 147
#MeToo movement, 47
Michigan State University, 37, 145
"mind the gap" warning, 1
Mitroff, Ian: *Managing Crises before They Happen,* 95

Nassar, Larry, 37, 38
National Incident Management System (NIMS), 55
nemawashi: concept of, 127

Occupy Wall Street movement, 57, 100
Only the Paranoid Survive (Moore), 46
ostrich organizations, 143, 144, 145, 151
over-optimism, 27-28, 117

peacock organizations, 144, 147-48, 151
presidents: bad news sharing, 130, 132; Board of Trustees and, 128, 129-30, 131; credibility of, 123;

crisis management involvement, 123-24, 132-35, 137, 138, 139-40; criticism of, 136, 138; decision-making abilities, 30-31, 133; faculty and, 126-27, 130; group dynamics and, 133; leadership of, 122, 131, 139-40; media relations and, 141; misplaced loyalty, 131; overconfidence of, 131; perception of leadership, 140; perils of the first-time, 136; presence on campus, 133; pressure on, 138; shared governance and, 124; stake-holder communications, 141; strategic priorities, 133-34; survival rate, 123
prevailing narratives, 108-9
protest management: defining roles in, 56-57; National Guard and, 57-58; operational and strategic priorities, 58, **59**; reputational impact of, 57-58; social media and, 100-101; violence and, 58

rankings criteria, 12
religious institutions: values of, 40
reporting criteria: clarity of, 44-45; cultural dependency of, 45; definition of, 43-44; "early warning" indicator role, 45; example of, **44**; reporting bar, 44-45; vertical communications in, 45
reputation: *vs.* brand, 13; building and ruining, 11-12, 25, 105; concept of, 2; damage to, 38, 109, 116-18; feedback loop, 7-8; protection of, 1-3, 11, 14; rankings and, 12; Socrates on, 7, 8, 11, 12